f. 30-63

P9-CQN-313

THE GOSPEL OF THE CROSS

THE GOSPEL
OF THE CROSS

A SECOND SERIES OF SERMONS

By

Karl Heim, Ph.D.,

*Professor of Systematic Theology in the
University of Tuebingen
Author of "The Living Fountain," etc.*

TRANSLATED BY
JOHN SCHMIDT, B.D.,
Pastor, Augsburg Lutheran Church, Detroit, Mich.

ZONDERVAN PUBLISHING HOUSE
GRAND RAPIDS   MICHIGAN

EIGHT-FIFTEEN FRANKLIN STREET
GRAND RAPIDS, MICHIGAN

To
JOHN O. EVJEN, PH.D.
PROFOUND SCHOLAR, INSPIRING TEACHER,
MAN OF FAITH
THIS TRANSLATION IS RESPECTFULLY DEDICATED.

TRANSLATOR'S PREFACE

THE STRENGTH of the Gospel of Christ lies in the Cross and in the Empty Tomb. In the former it faces honestly and boldly the tragedy of sin; in the latter it rises to the glory of victory. The preaching of Professor Karl Heim is Cross-centered. Unafraid he faces the fears, doubts and questionings of our modern age. In answer he presents the Gospel of the Cross.

A good sermon is both time-less and time-bound. It offers the ageless truth of an era that is continually in flux. It speaks from eternity into time. Thus the preacher must know, not only the Bible Message, but also the day to which he preaches. He must understand its essential strength and weakness even better than do those who live only for this life. He must pierce beneath the kaleidoscopic activity of life to find its true meaning. He must understand both the desires and the hungers of the human heart, if he is to present the Gospel effectively.

These sermons, preached in 1930 and 1931 to men and women facing a world much like our own, measure up to this test.

JOHN SCHMIDT.

Detroit, Michigan.

CONTENTS

I.
SCORNED LOVE

Hear another parable: There was a certain householder which planted a vineyard, and hedged it round about, and digged a winepress in it, and built a tower, and let it out to husbandmen, and went into a far country; And when the time of the fruit drew near, he sent his servants to the husbandmen, that they might receive the fruits of it. And the husbandmen took his servants, and beat one, and killed another, and stoned another. Again, he sent other servants more than the first: and they did unto them likewise. But last of all he sent unto them his son, saying, They will reverence my son. But when the husbandmen saw the son, they said among themselves, This is the heir; come let us kill him and let us seize on his inheritance. And they caught him, and cast him out of the vineyard, and slew him. When the lord therefore of the vineyard cometh, what will he do unto those husbandmen? They say unto him, He will miserably destroy those wicked men, and will let out his vineyard unto other husbandmen, which shall render him the fruits in their seasons. Jesus saith unto them, Did ye never read in the scriptures, The stone which the builders rejected, the same is become the head of the corner: this is the Lord's doing, and it is marvelous in our eyes? Therefore say I unto you, The kingdom of God shall be taken from you, and given to a nation bringing forth the fruits thereof.

MATTHEW 21:33-43

I.

SCORNED LOVE

ONE OF the bitter experiences that we have in this world is when someone for whom we have great affection and for whom we have made many sacrifices scorns our love. Tragic is the mother whose son, after he has moved to another city, entirely forgets his parental home in the excitement of new relationships. Her letters and her gifts bring no response. Those of us who have experienced this pain of scorned love, whether as mother, father, teacher or friend will understand why Hamlet, in the famous soliloquy in which he assembles all possible causes for suicide, if that were a true escape, should emphasize, "the pangs of despised love." But all this sorrow due to rejected love, which in a thousand varied forms fills the earth, is only a faint shadow of the tragedy of Jesus' parable. It tells the sorrow of One Who has spent His whole life in a desperate, unbroken and yet unsuccessful attempt to win the soul of His people. And now, just before His Passion, He is overcome with this tragedy. In Luke's Gospel we read: *And when He was come near, He beheld the city and wept over it.* And Matthew adds His words: *O Jerusalem, Jerusalem, thou that killest the prophets and stonest them which are sent unto thee, how often would I have gathered thy children together, even as a hen gathereth her chickens under her wings, and*

13

ye would not! Even, today, when one stands as a pilgrim on the Mount of Olives, where Jesus spoke this tragic word, it is as if it still trembles in the air. The whiteness of the Temple area still gleams in the sun, but the Temple itself is destroyed and the blue domes of a mosque rise in its stead. No Jew walks there lest he tread upon the Holy of Holies. *The kingdom of God shall be taken from you.* Jesus' words on this occasion were tragically fulfilled: *Thine enemies shall cast a trench about thee, and compass thee round, and keep thee in on every side, and shall lay thee even with the ground, and thy children within thee; and they shall not leave in thee one stone upon another because thou knewest not the time of thy visitation.*

The people of God, among whom He had worked many great deeds for more than a thousand years, in this decisive moment had rejected their King. Since that day the Jew wanders through all the earth, never finding a real home. But we who read this bit of history dare not permit ourselves to be stirred merely as we are stirred by a scene in a play. No; we participate in this history. We share in the responsibility for this tragedy of Jesus. For there is not one among us who has not, somewhere in his life, scorned the seeking love of God. The parable Jesus tells is the history of Israel; and yet, it is also our individual history. That is why we can read this parable only with deep humility as we consider:

1. How much love God has directed toward us;
2. How terrible it is when we repeatedly reject His seeking love.

I.

How much God has done to draw us to Himself! The Bible frequently compares God's work among men with a vineyard. Not with a rose garden that, in Southern lands, produces a large supply of blossoms with virtually no attention; nor with an oak forest, which needs no help to enable it to withstand storms. No; when God seeks a comparison for His work in the world, He selects a weak plant, the grapevine, that requires an enormous amount of human sweat and labor before, finally, in late autumn, it produces its ripe fruit. *There was a certain householder which planted a vineyard.* This has its first application to Israel. There God had established a congregation with a Temple in which daily sacrifice and prayer were offered to Him. This was the vineyard which God had planted in the midst of a fallen world. We must, however, apply it to ourselves as well. For Jesus, Himself, said that the Kingdom, which was first given to Israel, would be taken from them and given to the Gentiles. Since the day that Columba and Gallus, the Irish missionaries, entered our German forests, God's vineyard has been among us, also. In the heart of everyone who learned as a little child to pray and who has come within the power of God's Word, is planted a seed of eternity. Everyone who has come within the sound of God's thunderous words has received this tender plant. We can let it shrivel up or be surrounded by weeds, but we can never tear it out of our hearts. No one who

has tasted the honey of eternity can ever again have
his wants wholly satisfied by this world.

He knows that the greatest accomplishments of our
modern technical genius, that enables us to destroy distance, are totally worthless if the center of his life remains empty and dead. The most stimulating companionships are mere baubles when the seed, which God
has planted in us, receives no nourishment from them.
God has planted this seed in us; He also cares for it.
All the watchful attention of God is included in the
statement: *He hedged it round about, and digged a
winepress in it, and built a tower*—Jesus was perhaps
thinking, here, of the protection which the people had
enjoyed during the reign of David—*and let it out to
husbandmen, and went into a far country.* It is impossible to tell how much God has done for us that this
tender plant, which He gave us in childhood, should
be protected. We need mention but one. We still possess Sunday as a day of rest from our labor. It is a
sheltering power for the tender plant of our longing for
eternity. In Russia, the factories are being operated
on Sundays as on other days to aid in the attempt
being made to tear the last remnant of faith from the
Russian heart. But we still possess this day of silence,
when the wheels of industry stand still. Very much
misused it is, but we still have it. And we still have
the churches, in which those who have no opportunity
at home to be alone can gather for an hour to hear
sacred music and the divine Word, that is so much more
powerful than all human words. But all the attention
which God has given us, the sheltering hand which He

has placed over the tender plant of our soul, has a purpose. A vineyard does not exist to bring forth sweet-smelling blossoms. It fulfills its purpose and rewards all the labor bestowed upon it only when the ripe fruit is brought in amid the jubilant shouts of the husbandmen. All the care which God has for us has but one goal—when it is not attained all His efforts are in vain —that we, His creation, bring the fruits of our life to Him Whose we are. *Whosoever will save his life shall lose it: and whosoever will lose his life for My sake shall find it.* Each of us experiences at least a bit of this truth when he "loses" something of his life, perhaps a bit of his time, an evening or two in a week, or a bit of his strength, to help those whom God puts in his way.

Only recently, I heard of a young woman whose husband, upon whom her affection was centered, was taken from her, suddenly and under tragic circumstances. At first she thought that her life had lost all meaning, that it had become quite empty. She wanted to withdraw from the world and bury herself in selfish sorrow. Then the thought came to her, "I will give the remnant of my life, the wreck that is left, to my fellowmen. I will dedicate my life to the suffering, as a nurse." And then a new world opened to her. She found herself richer than she had been in earlier and more fortunate days. She realized that she had found her mission. Her fruit had ripened. There may be one among us whose life also is a wreck, beaten about by storms. But however, little we may have, if we are willing to lose this little for Christ's sake, we can become wealthy! Bodelschwingh angered many people by saying to his deaconesses and nurses, "What does it matter if you should die sooner than you would otherwise do? You are not here to reach a snug old age!" Yet what he said was true. It is not our mission in life to celebrate a comfortable old age. Had that been the case, God would not have placed us in a world where we are surrounded by many dangers and where the man who seeks to do his duty is given sleepless nights because of those for whom he feels himself responsible. We have a higher mission. We are to be like the grapevine on the mountainside, living in the heat of the burning sun until the day comes when its fruit has ripened. Even this is not the end. The ripe grape is cast into the winepress of God to be trodden under. Its valuable content must be surrendered entirely to the Owner. It is to accomplish this purpose in us that God has planted and nurtured the seed in our hearts.

But now God does something even more remarkable. *And when the time of the fruit drew near, he sent his servants to the husbandmen, that they might receive the fruits of it.* The lord of the vineyard might have taken the fruit, which belonged to him, by force. But he did not. He did not send his servants as the state sends tax collectors, under the protection of the police. There would, in that case, been no further happenings. But he sends them utterly without defense! They are to request that the husbandmen surrender that which belongs to their master. In this lies the greatness of God's dealing with us. He, Who could destroy us any moment and take from us everything that we have, seeks our willing surrender. The full fruition of our lives is possible only when we willingly surrender them to Him. A compulsory service, such as that which might be forced from a child, is quite worthless in God's sight. It is the very opposite of that which God desires. That is why, although He possesses the power to compel us, that God seeks our willing surrender. He sends defenseless servants to ask for the fruits of the vineyard.

All the prophets whom God has sent were exposed to human wrath. Jeremiah could not protect himself against those who threw him into a dungeon, where he sank into the mire. John the Baptist had no protection when his head was laid upon the block because a king was offended by the truth. This made possible the frightful continuation of the parable: *And the husbandmen took his servants, and beat one, and killed another, and stoned another.* Every human owner of a vineyard would have sent for the police immediately, that the murderers should be punished and then he would have taken the yield of his land by force. But God does something that is beyond our understanding. He comes once more to those who have murdered His servants. Once again He seeks the love of these murderers. *Again, he sent other servants more than the first.* How far God descends to us! How greatly He must have desired us, that He should have done something so completely impossible in human eyes! If a beggar, who had come to our door and had there been given a costly gift, were to throw it upon the ground and should go away cursing, we would slam the door behind him and say, "I will never again have anything

to do with such a person! My patience is exhausted.
I haven't a cent to spare for such a worthless fellow.
He will never cross my threshold again. Surely He
doesn't expect me to run after him!"

But God is greater than the impatient human heart.
Did He not possess this patience—that leads Him to
come again and again to those who have rejected Him,
—not one of us would be saved! Perhaps it was in
our childhood that He came to us for the first time;
but then came the days when we were proud of our
youthful strength, and we thought, "Only a weakling
prays." Proudly we rejected His invitation. He might
then have permitted us to be lost, but He did not. He
came again, perhaps in more mature years, but this
time His approach is more powerful. He wounded us
with a blow from which we cannot soon recover. Or
perhaps He sent us someone who made an unforgettable
impression upon us. What marvelous patience, that
we should read here, *He sent other servants!*

And they did unto them likewise. Now, surely,
run our thoughts, even God's patience must come to an
end. Surely He will destroy these rebels. But Luther
says, somewhere, "If someone would draw a picture of
God, He must draw one of pure love, as though the
divine nature were a great fiery furnace of love that
fills the heaven and the earth." The double rejection
makes possible the supreme deed of mercy. Here we
come to the most crucial point of our parable, in which
Jesus gives us a glimpse into the ultimate mystery of
God's grace: *Then said the lord of the vineyard, What
shall I do? I will send my beloved son: it may be they*

will reverence him when they see him. So runs Luke's account. God reasons with Himself what He shall do. His prophets are dead, they have been murdered, stoned or burned. He has only one treasure left, the last and most precious. *I will send my beloved son.* Perhaps they will repent when they see that I have made this supreme sacrifice. Perhaps that will win them. Perhaps that will cause even the cruelest to say, "We cannot withstand such goodness. It is utterly undeserved. We will cease our rebellion against Him." All of us who have been reared within the influence of the church experience a moment when the statement, *I will send my beloved son,* is fulfilled in us individually. It is the moment when Jesus, in all His purity and majesty, comforts our soul. A modern author, not a Christian, has said, "Once in his life each of us must go with Him from Jerusalem to Emmaus." This writer means that a time comes for every man when he must say, *Did not our hearts burn within us, while He talked with us . . . ?* When that moment comes we join the multitude of husbandmen to whom the Owner of the vineyard has given His ultimate gift, those to whom He has given His Son that they might do with Him what they will. This gives to our lives a divine possibility! Possibly, when we see Him, we will repent. Possibly we will be ashamed to raise our hand against Him. Possibly this supreme gift will silence our criticism. It is of great importance to God that, at this moment, He bring no pressure to bear upon us. He might have sent Christ as a ruler, with the support of legions of angels. He might have sent fire from heaven, as in the days of

Elisha. That would have made it appear as though God wished to compel us to bow before Him. But the Son comes to us quite weaponless, and *went about doing good, and healing all that were oppressed of the devil.* He sits down with publicans and sinners, the outcasts of society, whom everyone avoids. His holy hand touches those who suffer from the most loathsome diseases. He prays for the disciples who, from sheer cowardice, would betray and deny Him. He replies to hatred, spite and unfaithfulness only with love. *I will send my beloved son.*

II.

When we look back and consider everything that God has done for us—how He has planted the seed of childhood faith within us; how He guarded it with His protecting hand; how He sent messenger after messenger to us to remind us of the fruit we owe Him; and how, finally, He gave His most costly gift, His beloved Son, we are overwhelmed at the fulness of His grace. How terrible it is if we reject all this! But we say that *we* have *not* been guilty of this! We shudder at the abyss of those who, like the husbandmen say, *This is the heir: come, let us kill him, and let us seize on his inheritance.* Our moral sense revolts against the Jewish leaders who sought to retain their hold upon the religious life of the people and therefore rejected Him Whom God sent. But there is something worse than this brutal act of the Jews. Their barbarous action was, at least, an indication that they took Jesus seriously. They knew that they could not endure His presence un-

less a fundamental change occurred in their lives. That
is why they killed Him.

But there is another, a more reprehensible treat-
ment of Jesus! And that is the one of which we are
so frequently guilty. It consists in the cold indifference
with which, again and again, we confront Him. Doubt-
less we know very accurately the things in our lives
which must be surrendered if the fruit, which God demands of us, is to be forthcoming. Possibly God has
been reminding us for years of some particular thing
which must be changed or dropped. But, although we
have been attending church frequently, we continue to
meet His demands with total indifference. We listen
to the preaching of His Gospel, but, inwardly, we remain unchanged. If we are guilty of such indifference,
the parable that we are studying speaks to us in words
of terrific earnestness! For Jesus tells us that the com-
ing of the Son is the *last* word which God can speak
to us. More than that He cannot give He cannot send
a more urgent invitation than that He should place before us His most precious possession to be the possible
object of our abuse and criticism. If, after this, we
still withstand Him, there remains for us only the judgment with which Jesus threatened the Jews. *Therefore, say I unto you, the Kingdom of God shall be
taken from you and given to a nation bringing forth
the fruits thereof.*

For God does not need us for the building of His
Kingdom. If we reject the Stone of stumbling, if the
builders of peoples and nations, the elders of the Jews
or the leaders of our own people, reject Christ, then

God can build His glorious temple upon this rejected
Cornerstone entirely without our aid. The train may
pass us by and we remain as we were, having missed
an opportunity. That God, even today, can find nations
that will bring their fruits to Him, is shown by a glance
at the mission fields. It shames us to enter a poverty
stricken village in India and to see how eagerly the
message of salvation is received. Between huts built
of mud and palm-leaves, the homes of outcasts who
live in inexpressible poverty and absolute dependence
upon the rich landowners, there stands a small church,
a straw-roofed "grace hut." When the director of our
Basel mission enters he sees a tightly packed congregation of men and women, whose faces reveal their
misery but who, nevertheless, have a wonderful gleam
in their eyes. Then an old fakir rises to say, "I too was
a lost sheep, a lost coin lying in the filth of demon-wor-
ship; yet, in the dreadful pit, the Good Shepherd found
me, and now I am free!" When we have had such an experience, whether in India or Africa, we know that God
does not need our people and our church to build His
Kingdom upon the earth. If we reject Jesus as a Stone
unsuited to our purpose, the Kingdom will be taken from
us and *given to a nation bringing forth the fruits thereof.*

The vineyard of God is still with us. We are still
surrounded by an overwhelming abundance of His gifts.
God grant that the study of this parable may lead us to
say, in the stillness of our prayer, to Him Who has
done so much for us, "Thou hast given me too much
that I should reject Thee. Thou art too great for me
and hast overcome me. I am Thine!"

II.

DEATH, AN ENEMY

Now there was at Joppa a certain disciple named Tabitha, which by interpretation is called Dorcas: this woman was full of good works and almsdeeds which she did. And it came to pass in those days that she was sick and died: whom when they had washed, they laid her in an upper chamber. And forasmuch as Lydda was nigh to Joppa, and the disciples heard that Peter was there, they sent unto him two men, desiring him that he would not delay to come to them. Then Peter arose and went with them. When he was come, they brought him into the upper chamber: and all the widows stood by him weeping and shewing the coats and garments which Dorcas made while she was with them. But Peter put them all forth, and kneeled down and prayed; and turning him to the body said, Tabitha, arise. And she opened her eyes: and when she saw Peter she sat up. And he gave her his hand and lifted her up, and when he had called the saints and widows, presented her alive. And it was known throughout all Joppa; and many believed in the Lord.

ACTS 9:36-42

II.

DEATH, AN ENEMY

OUR TEXT reveals how death broke, as an enemy, into a congregation of Christians and, also, how this early Christian Church faced the enemy. Let us consider these two facts, for we moderns can learn much from them both.

I.

Death is not a liberator but an enemy which the Church of Christ must face. That is the first fact which our text reveals. In Bernard's *Satan's Sun,* a book that has been read in hundreds of thousands of copies throughout Europe, there is a nerve-wracking scene that is a ghastly companion-piece to Luke's story. A priest stands at the foot of a bier upon which lies the corpse of a boy, whose life had meant a great deal to him. Candlelight flickers upon the pallid countenance. At his head stands a large cross. Now this priest attempts something superhuman. He takes the small body in both arms and elevates it before the cross. For a moment he thinks that the corpse begins to quiver and breathe. Then he hears behind him a horrible scream and mocking laughter. The dead body sinks back upon the bier, as the priest rushing from the room like a thief, flees directly through the gardens and across the

27

fields until he is back in the shadow of the village
church where he collapses.

Every time that a young man, in the midst of
youth's promises, is suddenly taken away, or when, as
in our text, an highly valued member of the congregation suddenly dies, it is as though we hear this mocking
laughter. We sense, then, that the Bible is right when
it speaks of death as *the last enemy*. In such cases
it is as though we hear death say, "Yes, rattle your
chains! Beat your fists until they bleed in your futile
effort to escape from the prison in which I hold you!
Use all your powers of intelligence and determination
in hospitals and laboratories to keep for a little while
those you fondly imagine belong to *you*, but who, in
reality, belong to *me!* Finally, they will still become
my prey. Ultimately, all your thoughts and wishes
and hopes, everything that you have achieved in this
life, will collapse like a house of cards when the wind
of my breath shall blow! I play with you for a time,
just as a cat plays with a mouse. I let you run here
and there, and pursue happiness, power and pleasure.
But it is only a brief game, you play. In the end, you
will, nevertheless, be mine!

We do not become so sharply conscious of the fact
that death is an enemy when a person, whose life work
has been completed, is gathered in like a sheaf of ripe
grain. A revealing light shines upon such an end. But
such cases are becoming increasingly rare in our day.
Someone has estimated that in our modern technical
age only a sixth of the population dies from natural
causes. Death shows its true nature when a man is

seized in the very midst of life. Here is a mother snatched away from her children who greatly need her help and counsel. There is a young man, for whose education his parents have taken the bread from their own mouths, taken just as he is about to assume his place in the world. Here is a missionary, educated by the sacrificial offerings of some little church and sent into a foreign country. Scarcely has his work begun when he falls victim to some malignant disease or the equatorial climate. Every time such a case occurs we attempt to comfort ourselves by saying, "It is a good thing for him; he has been spared much trouble." Yet we know that all this is but weak comfort. We cannot understand such occurrences. We are saddened and dismayed.

Such a disturbing experience was suffered by the congregation at Joppa by the sudden death of Tabitha. Luke's brief description gives us a clear picture of her. Then, as now, the most important members of the Church were not those who possessed the most knowledge — although we need them, also — nor were they those who made the most eloquent speeches; though eloquence is a valuable gift. Rather they are those unknown persons, whose doings are not publicly recorded, but from whom comes a helping strength which binds an entire congregation together. We are not told a single word which Tabitha said. We read only, *There was at Joppa a certain disciple named Tabitha, which by interpretation is called Dorcas (Gazelle).* She was well named, since she was swift to reach the place where sorrow had entered, where, perhaps, a mother was sick and unable herself to keep her children's clothes in repair. At once, Tabitha was there. Just as a fire engine is prepared immediately to rush to a burning house, so Tabitha was ready to go at once to places where help was needed. *This woman was full of good works and almsdeeds which she did.* These were not her vocation, a pleasure for her spare moments. She was not like the average member of a welfare association who gives an occasional spare hour to its work. No, she was full of good works and almsdeeds which filled her entire life and thought.

She was one of those rare women, of whom our own day knows a few. She might have said of herself what Eva von Tiele Winkler writes in her memoirs, "At the age of eighteen, life, with all its possibilities, lay before me. What would it bring? Happiness, love, satisfaction, riches, earthly joy, a brilliant career in society. None of these appealed to me. For I had had a glimpse of the world's need, of the misery of the poor, and therefore I desired but one thing, only one thing: to throw myself and everything that I was and had into the needs of our day; to give my aid to all who stood in solitude and forsakenness, in poverty and guilt." It matters not whether such a person has such large resources that he can finance great institutions of mercy, or lives in a lonely room. Wherever he is he forms the hidden center of a congregation. Around such an one there comes into being a whole family of needy ones, gathered like children about their mother. It is a circle of those who can again believe that there exists in the world something besides class struggle, class hatred, exploitation, and greed. One such person, even though he has no money, is worth more than a hundred books written in defense of the Christian faith. He is worth more than all the political lectures intended to show that class hatred cannot solve our problems, ever delivered!

And now we read, *It came to pass in those days, that she was sick and died.* In a single night, death extinguished the flame at which so many had warmed themselves. The church felt the presence of an enemy. It saw that this enemy does not merely affect our physical lives, but destroys also the bonds of love that have been woven between individuals. It threatens the inner life of the congregation. Its consequences go still further. When such an experience comes, it brings with it the thought — as Christians we scarcely dare entertain it, yet it comes, nevertheless—; if this is the end, so that Tabitha is now laid aside after a short period of activity and if nothing remains of her work except a few garments which she has sewed and a few hearts that sorrow at her passing, was all her effort and sacrifice really worth while. For what remains? Nothing more than when a flower which has stood for a time in a room, is carried out. For a little while the perfume lingers, but soon that, too, is gone. Would it not be better if we used our short life to the full? When Death, the reaper, pitilessly destroys many promising, young lives, as we observed him do during the Great War and as he does in tubercular sanitoriums, the result is not that people become the more serious-minded. The very opposite is true; they take life more lightly when the black shadow of death stands beside them. They say, "Why deny oneself of pleasures that can be had? 'Puck the rose, ere it wither!" *Let us eat, drink and be merry, for tomorrow we die.*

Thus we see that death is not a friend and deliverer. The Bible is right. It is *the last enemy.* It is not content merely to destroy our bodies, in order that the released soul may wing upward, as idealists say. No, it threatens our whole being, not only our physical life, but also our faith and our love! Whenever we see someone die, we observe that death destroys not only the life but attempts to destroy the soul as well. It has frequently occurred that sincere Christians, who have maintained their faith throughout a long life, are brought by death into the valley of doubt.

II.

This leads us to the second lesson of our text. We must ask the further question: How did this early company of believers overcome the dread enemy? What weapons were used to oppose him? The attitude of the congregation in Joppa seems strange to us, because we are accustomed to ground our arms in the presence of death, to offer him no opposition whatever. When death destroys a life we know of but two possible attitudes of mind. The first is that of spiritless renunciation: "Everything must end. Even the beautiful and the attractive are, in reality, vanity and nothingness." The other is a yearning for death. "Come sweet death." We hear this note in the funeral liturgies of the Buddhists: "For-

tunate one! The spring and autumn of your life is past,
while we must struggle on."

But the incident we are considering overcomes both
altitudes. We are impressed, not merely by what Peter
did but also with the action of the whole congregation
of the church at Joppa. They did not go moodily through
the streets to make preparations for an impressive
funeral. They saw that there was still another possibility. It was in the air, even though they did not express it, and in accordance with it they acted. They
did not bury the body of Tabitha but laid it in an upper
room. Then they sent two messengers who made the
three-hour journey to Peter in Lydia. These messengers
made no appeal, but Peter understood what they meant
and returned with them to Joppa. When he entered the
house and heard the wailing of the widows; when he
encountered the whole atmosphere of sorrow and
despair, he refused to be conquered by it but threw—
for so the Scripture reads literally—the weeping women
out of the house and knelt down. He refused to let
these crippling and depressing influences work their will
on him. He wished to be entirely alone with God that
he might see what God would do. He did not know
what God might do, but he knew that He might do something altogether astonishing! While he prayed he was
given to see that he, sinful Peter, dared to use almost
the same words as those which Jesus had used in the
house of Jairus, whose little daughter had died: *Damsel,
I say unto thee, arise!* And now Peter said, *Tabitha,
arise!* God heard this prayer and something occurred
which was so amazing and majestic that no one thought

to honor Peter or to praise him as the conqueror of
death, but, as the account reads, *Many believed in the
Lord.*

We know that, in our day, such miracles rarely
occur. In that first period of revelation a path had to
be blazed by means of startling events. Mountains had
to be blasted. During the succeeding centuries the
stream of Christian faith has worn such a deep canyon
for itself that such mighty deeds are no longer necessary. But still we must ask how it was possible that
people just as weak as ourselves, who knew as well as
we the power of death, should, in such a situation, not
surrender, but recognize that there was the possibility
of a triumphant miracle? To this question we must
answer that this congregation of the church at Joppa
which still lived in their first love to the Savior, knew
something which we have almost forgotten—something
which we must learn anew. It knew that since our Lord
had died upon the cross and had been raised again from
the dead, the authority of death had reached its end.
Since that day the power of death is conquered. We
need no longer surrender before him. There is no more
reason for a dreary renunciation of life or for a yearning for death! We can approach this last enemy with
head held high. For what we read in the First Epistle
of John is true: *The life was manifested and we have
seen it and bear witness, and show unto you that eternal
life, which was with the Father and was manifested unto
us.* We do not have to wait for a future conquest of
death. The victory is already won. The might of this
last enemy already is broken!

Why is this true? Paul has written, *The sting of death is sin.* There *is*, then, a weapon by means of which death keeps us in subjection, like the cruel goad, in earlier days, was used to control oxen. What is this weapon with which death conquers us? It is not the frailty of our bodies, nor the danger of contagion through the bacilli of which we are so much afraid. These are but external expressions for something much more important. The weapon of death is the burden of unforgiven guilt. From our own experience we know what Paul meant by this hideous word. So long as there is a burden upon our conscience—a lie we have not corrected, a stolen article we have not returned, a false oath we have sworn—we cannot think of death without fear. Sometimes when a fire breaks out in a barn the horses are not released in time. So they plunge madly in an attempt to break loose. Even so does death hold a man in its power, when the conscience is not set free. But now Christ has destroyed these bonds! Through that which He suffered, He has set our conscience free! We need only to flee to Golgotha, the one place where the Destroyer cannot overpower us. Redemption is possible for everyone who makes his way there in faith. Through His death Christ has taken from the enemy's hand the only weapon by which he can maintain his power over us.

Death is still here, of course. We still suffer bodily infirmity; but the *might* of death is forever destroyed! It is as though we lived in an enemy-occupied territory after the command has been given that the foreign troops return home. The whole land breathes freely.

The departure of the soldiers may occupy some time; many days may elapse before the last soldier is gone. But in the moment in which the command for evacuation is given all fear of the foreign power is done away. Its authority is gone. Wherever and whenever the peace of God's forgiveness enters a human heart, the power of death is broken. The man stands, not on the side of death, but on the side of life! Hence, we are able to understand why this early congregation felt it possible that God could exercise His power over death, through a human agent.

How does this incident affect our attitude toward death? The power of death and destruction approach us from every side. We are threatened as individuals and as a people. Just recently a man said to me on the street, after reading the latest newspaper headlines, "I have no more hope for Germany. We have signed our own death warrant!" And it is true that, when we observe conditions about us, it would seem as though the very air we breathe is being taken away. Death does not threaten us from the outside only. It comes also from within, through those plagues which attack the very marrow of our national life. In our cities nearly every tenth person is a carrier of this deadly evil. In the condition which today confronts our people there can be but two groups of men. On the one side stand those who have lost hope. Their cry is, "Nothing more can be done; Communism will come and destroy us!" On the other side, stand those who still hope. On which side do we, as Christians, stand? Not on the side of death, but on the side of life. Not because we believe in the inexhaustible strength of the German people, for this faith is completely shattered. Not because we believe there is something good and fine in every man; it would be difficult—if not impossible—to maintain this belief any longer. There is but one basis for our confidence. As Christians we can do what Peter did when he entered a house filled with the tragedy of death and in which he heard the weeping of those who had lost hope. He refused to be affected by these things, but sought a place where he could be alone and speak with God. And this place is open to us, also. Whenever we truly pray we stand at the place from which the whole world can be moved. Every morning, before he enters upon the difficult tasks of his occupation, or at eventide when he once more surveys the problems confronting him each of us can enter the place where the Resurrected One waits, where he can be alone with God Who is Lord over life and death! There he may know that death is conquered. God's final conquest over the power of death is assured. No longer need we be troubled or afraid. Life has the ultimate word!

It is because we have this place of power into which we may enter that Christians can participate so effectively in the endeavors of those who seek to maintain individual and national life. The world has often wondered why Christian men and women, who place so much emphasis upon the future life, should attend the blind, crippled and feeble-minded with such self-forgetful devotion; that they should be the best nurses in institutions for incurables. Only recently, a physician emphasized his conviction that Christian deaconesses, appraised from a purely professional point of view, were the best possible nurses. What is the reason for it? It is not sympathy, alone. There is a more fundamental cause. Christians know that every life is precious, for it comes from God. They know, too, that even the most miserable life contains the germ of a great eternity. For death is not the end. We do not pass into nothingness; we confront life. Therefore, the Christian's yearning for death is something quite different from that of the Buddhist's. Yes, we also long for death, at times. Not, however, because we love death; not because we fear death; not because we desire to be lost in nothingness, but because we desire LIFE! It is difficult, sometimes, for us to await its beginning. Therefore, we yearn for death with Paul's yearning, *I have a desire to depart, and to be with Christ, which is far better.*

III.

A LUKEWARM CHURCH

And unto the angel of the church of the Laodiceans write: These things saith the Amen, the faithful and true witness, the beginning of the creation of God; I know thy works, that thou art neither cold nor hot: I would that thou wert cold or hot. So then because thou art lukewarm, and neither cold nor hot, I will spue thee out of my mouth. Because thou sayest, I am rich and increased with goods and have need of nothing; and knowest not that thou art wretched and miserable, and poor, and blind, and naked: I counsel thee to buy of Me gold tried in the fire, that thou mayest be rich; and white raiment, that thou mayest be clothed, and that the shame of thy nakedness do not appear; and anoint thine eyes with eyesalve, that thou mayest see. As many as I love, I rebuke and chasten: be zealous, therefore, and repent. Behold, I stand at the door, and knock: if any man hear My voice and open the door, I will come in to him, and will sup with him, and he with Me. To him that overcometh will I grant to sit with Me in My throne, even as I also overcame and am set down with My Father in His throne. He that hath an ear, let him hear what the Spirit saith unto the churches.

REVELATION 3:14-22.

III.

A LUKEWARM CHURCH

THE SEVEN letters of the *Book of Revelation* are among the most precious possessions of the church. For in them we do not merely hear the Lord Jesus address His disciples. Here the Ascended One speaks to His church as represented in these seven congregations. What He has to say about the church is surely of far greater importance than the decisions of a synodical convention or the resolutions of an international church congress. The seer of *Revelation* tells how he received these letters. During a vision he heard a trumpet behind him and then a voice *as the sound of many waters*, one that shut out all human voices and all earthly sounds. When we stand at the side of an open grave and listen to the memorial addresses of lodges and fraternities that exalt the merits of the departed dead, we are impressed with the fact that while all this may be very consoling for relatives and friends, yet for him who has now entered eternity these voices are unimportant. Praises and criticisms, all the gossip about him in town, everything written about him in newspapers and books, has suddenly become insignificant and he hears but one voice, *as the sound of many waters*, the voice of Him before Whom all of us must, sooner or later stand and Who alone can give final judgment over our

lives. *These things saith the Amen,* writes John. By
which he means that in Him all promises are fulfilled,
that His "Amen" is indispensable to our life. *The faithful and true witness,* whose word is certain, the *beginning of the creation of God,* in Whom the entire creation
plan of God is gathered together. It is He alone Who
can say of Himself, *I know thy works.* What does He,
Who alone has the right to judge, say of the church?
Every one of His words has eternal significance. We
have here a judgment of Christ concerning a Christian
church that is not entirely unlike our own. Like us, she
had a rich spiritual inheritance. She had peace without for she suffered no persecution. What had Jesus to
say of such a church?

Let us note the two aspects of His judgment. He
speaks, first, of the deadly danger that threatens the
church. *I would that thou wert cold or hot. So then
because thou art lukewarm, and neither cold or hot, I
will spue thee out of my mouth.* And in the second
place He speaks of the unlimited wealth of the church.
*Behold, I stand at the door and knock: if any man hear
My voice and open the door, I will come in to him, and
will sup with him and he with Me. He that hath an ear,
let him hear what the Spirit saith unto the churches.*

I.

Our day has a new appreciation for the church.
Especially is this true of our youth. When, today, we
sing the old chorales that were born of the turmoil of
the Reformation and Thirty Years' War, we seem to
hear joining us the voices of those who first sang these
great hymns. British soldiers have related the deep

impression made upon them at the beginning of the
World War when German troops marched forward
singing, "A Mighty Fortress is our God." It seemed as
though this were the militant church of God. They
hesitated to turn their machine guns against them. And
now we are again learning what a treasure we have in
the chorales of Luther. And when we read the majestic
language of Luther's translation of the Bible, it seems
as though the spirits of those who clung to these words
in distress and death, who received all their power from
these words, are praying with us. But just when we are
rejoicing in this new appreciation of the church, we are
startled by this word of Christ. It is directed to a church
which felt itself much richer than we feel ourselves, one
that could truly say of itself, *I am rich and increased
with goods and have need of nothing.* The church of
Laodicea stood very near the Apostolic era—as near as
we stand to the Franco Prussian War, some of whose
veterans still live in Tuebingen. This congregation still
lived in the shadow of the great apostles, John and
Peter. So it was not to humanists, not to casual by-
standers, not to former church members that Jesus
spoke. This startling word was addressed to a congregation having an exceedingly great heritage. *I know thy
works, that thou art neither cold nor hot: I would that
thou wert cold or hot. So then because thou art lukewarm, and neither cold nor hot, I will spue thee out of
my mouth.*

With these words Christ says that which no pastor
would dare to say, if the Lord had not Himself spoken,
that if we do not surrender to Him with hot, glowing

hearts, it is much better that we remain ice-cold and become an Antichrist like Nietzsche or the Bolsheviks. When a thirsty traveler in the Orient comes to an inn, he is offered hot water, tea or else cold water fresh from the spring; but lukewarm water that has been standing about is not endurable. Why does the Lord use such a crushing illustration to picture lukewarm Christians, who have had a certain religious fervor but has lost most of it? Are not these the very people whom we regard so highly? They are the ones who are stimulated by a sermon, who enjoy religious discussions and have a certain appreciation of the value of religion. They do not reject Christianity, but they refuse to make a clean break with those things which the world has to offer. They are frequently the most agreeable companions, for with them one can discuss any subject. Why should Jesus say of them, "I will spit them out like stale water" It is because this is not a matter of any human relationship, but of our relationship to God. If it were a matter of some earthly business, possibly some artistic program, one could say, "I am willing to give part of my time to this cause, say, one evening a week. That is not enough to make me an accomplished artist but it will have to do."

But when we stand before God the situation is entirely different. Then we stand before One Who completely surrounds us and to Whom every breath of our life belongs. *Whatsoever is under the whole heaven is Mine*, we read in *Job*. When we withhold part of our life from God it is just as bad, perhaps even worse, than if we should rise in open rebellion against Him. Either

we must make a complete surrender of ourselves to Him
or we must say with Nietzsche, "God is dead." But if I
think that I can conclude some pacific understanding
with God by which I can dedicate a few hours of my life
to Him while retaining the rest in my own hand, my
action is more reprehensible than open rebellion. For
then I do not even recognize that I am dealing with *God*.
That is why Jesus says that an ice-cold atheist is prefer-
able to a lukewarm confessor of Christianity. When a
train leaves the station there are frequently belated passengers who might still leap aboard the moving train.
But the station attendant will not permit this. Why not?
Because such an attempt to board a moving train is dangerous. One might succeed in swinging aboard safely.
But failure would result in his injury and possible death.
This is a parable illustrating what occurs when we go
to church and come in contact with the eternal powers
that flow forth from the crucified Christ. This is a dangerous proceeding. If it leads to a complete surrender,
all is well. Then we are carried along through death to
the eternal world by the power of Christ's redemptive
death. We are borne safely into eternity, when we en-
trust ourselves to Him. But when this does not occur
our contact with the living power will hurl us away and
we will suffer grave injury. *I will spue thee out of my
mouth*, says Jesus.

The triumphal march of Christ through the world is
marked by the presence of those who have been cast to
earth because they did not find full entrance into His
Kingdom. They were smitten as was Uzzah when he
touched the ark of God. Frequently the most bitter

enemies of the cross of Christ have come from the most dedicated Christian families, in which daily worship was observed. Why? They came into close contact with the power of prayer, but they would not take the step by which they could enter into the fellowship of Christ. Because of this failure they were flung back. For there is but one way to experience the power of the Crucified and that is the way to which Christ points when He says, *I would thou wert hot.* That means that we must be filled completely with gratitude and joy. We can be *hot* spiritually, only when we no longer belong to ourselves but have completely surrendered to Him.

All of us have a desire to give ourselves, without restraint, to something beyond ourselves. This desire is much stronger in us than the desire for happiness. Only when we have found something for which we can give ourselves, do we really live. Only then does the great stream of life pass through us and start to glow as do electric bulbs when the current passes through them. Then we become young. Only in this way can we be freed from the petty cares of the everyday. If this stream does not pass through our hearts, we destroy ourselves. Our heart revolts against itself, like an imprisoned beast which wounds itself against the bars of its own cage.

There are but two kinds of people, those who have found that which gives meaning to their lives, for which they would be willing to be destroyed, and those who are still in restless search for life's purpose. If we cannot find an eternal purpose for life, we must find a temporal one for which we are ready to live and die.

This we may find in a political party or in a blind loyalty to some person. For all of us feel that our fast-fading life has meaning only when we surrender ourselves to a cause or person greater than ourselves. Everything else, all the pleasures and joys that life offers, are as impermanent as spring blossoms.

And Jesus says that God and His Word, which alone can supply meaning to our lives, can be approached only by those who are willing to make a complete surrender, who come with the fervent wish to be filled entirely by Him. If we come in any other way—as, say, with a desire to be entertained—then our church attendance, our hearing of the Word and our reception of the Lord's Supper are an insurrection against God. It would be far better if we remained outside. Christ will spue us from His mouth as a man would lukewarm water. The decisive thing is not whether we have much to give, a rich life or a youthful heart; God asks only if it is all that we have, if we are bringing everything to Him. Jesus once called the attention of His disciples to the poor widow who cast her mites into the Temple treasury, and said, *This poor widow hast cast more in, than all they which have cast into the treasury: for all they did cast in out of their abundance; but she of her want did cast in all that she had . . .*

Many of us are like the poor widow; we have not much to give. One has only a wearied body; another has but a short span of years; another's circle of influence includes but a single person. I know a woman who found a blind child and lived to care for and educate this child; while her own life became great and beautiful. It may be that some cannot do even this much. Perhaps there are those who can do no more than to speak a few friendly words. In the eyes of Jesus it does not matter if we have much or little to give, if only it can be said of us "that of our want we cast in all that we had." The friendly look, the small gift or the faithfulness with which we do our "unimportant" tasks are acceptable to God when they represent a complete surrender, so that we can say, "I have given everything which I have."

But do we do this? Do we do this even in the few hours which we spend together in church? Do not these words of Jesus contain a judgment upon many of the things which we do together, even there? We dare to sing the Church's great hymns of faith. We venture to sing,

> *Thee will I love, till the pure fire*
> *Fill my whole soul with chaste desire.*

And even as we sing, our thoughts are busied with last evening's party or with the pleasure-drive that we have planned for the afternoon. We dare to pray that prayer which Jesus taught His disciples, men who had left everything to follow Him—we dare to say, *Thy will be done*, even though we know very well that we are not willing to surrender certain questionable practices in our lives. We venture to present a child for baptism and too often this baptism is only the occasion for a family celebration, ending in careless merrymaking. And we dare to offer this to God who sees everything that we are! Is that not dreadful? Must Christ not spue us from His mouth? Would it not, in many cases,

be far more honorable to remain entirely outside the
pale of his church along with those who profess no relationship to Him? Christ cannot endure one who is one
sort of a person in church and another in the beer garden and dance hall. He will spue such out of His mouth.

Perhaps all of us have become conscious of the
danger that confronts us,—the danger of making light
of sacred things and lulling ourselves into the sleep of
self-satisfaction. *Thou sayest,* says the Lord, *I am rich,
and increased with goods, and have need of nothing;
and knowest not that thou art wretched and miserable,
and poor, and blind, and naked.* In other words, your
wealth is fictitious. You are *wretched,* even though
others praise you as a faithful member of the church.
You are *blind,* though you are regarded as an authority
in the field of religion, since you lack the eyes that
would enable you to understand it. You are miserable
and naked and are frozen inwardly, though the warm
stream of life passes near you. *I counsel thee to buy of
Me gold,* that is, that you act as though you had nothing,
like one whose home is burned and who must again buy
the necessities of life. Buy *white raiment, that thou
mayest be clothed, and that the shame of thy nakedness
do no appear; and anoint thine eyes with eyesalve, that
thou mayest see.*

II.

Thus far our text has brought us only the tremendous words that Christ addresses to His cold congregation. But perhaps the very reading of the text called
our attention to the fact that suddenly an entirely new
tone was heard. It is as though one comes out of the

cold dampness of a cavern, into which he wandered during a hike, into the warm air of spring. Jesus says, *As many as I love, I rebuke and chasten: be zealous, therefore, and repent.* So even this sharp expression of spueing from the mouth comes from a Savior Who loves His church! He seeks to revive even a dead churchianity by means of His mercy. Here is the most precious fact in this epistle to an indifferent church. Long experience justifies the belief that there is nothing more difficult to arouse to life than a lukewarm church. Heathen who have never heard the message of the Gospel are frequently easier to reach. Utschimura, a Japanese Christian, tells that he went singing through the streets when the truth dawned upon him that there was but one God, and not a multitude of deities. Such was his joy when he learned this basic truth of the Bible. In Indo-China a tribe of cannibals staged a war-dance before the missionary to show him their joy at having heard the story of Jesus. The children of the desert thirst for the water of life. But when one has heard the Gospel of Jesus from childhood, when year after year the festivals of the church pass by him, when the Crucified had been pictured repeatedly before his eyes, and when there has been no consequent surrender of his heart, we become partially "immune" to these powerful impressions. But here the boundless mercy of Jesus shows itself. His love is so great that it can break through even the strongest barrier, the barrier of a dead churchianity.

What is the treasure that even a dead church of Christ still possesses? The wealth of the church does not consist in vast cathedrals nor in the majestic notes of

organs. Its wealth is summed up in the words, *Behold,
I stand at the door and knock: if any man hear My
voice and open the door, I will come in to him, and will
sup with him and he with Me.* We have excluded Him
by our lukewarmness. We have thrown the bolt that we
might prevent His entrance into our lives. But still He
has not given us up. The barred-out Savior knocks at
the door. He knows that we cannot continue indefinitely
in this separation. We do not read that He breaks in
the door. He will not compel nor overmaster. Jesus
desires us to retain our liberty. He seeks a surrender
born of complete liberty and clear understanding. He
can dwell only in a heart which willingly dedicates itself to Him. He stands waiting at the door to make a
last attempt to win us. *I knock*, are the works He uses.
In the original the word signifies, not a loud sound, but
a touch, as of a musician on his lyre, or as an intended
buyer in the market place, tapping a piece of pottery to
discover if it be sound. Jesus knocks softly upon the
door. There is not one of us who has not already heard
this soft knocking. We hear it in the beating of our
hearts that remind us that they will not always beat. We
hear it in the stroke of the fleeting hours that herald the
approach of eternity. We hear it in the voice of conscience, when we cannot sleep and everything about us
is still, as silent as it will be in eternity when life is
over and we look back upon that which we have done or
not done in this mortal life. We hear it in the Holy
Scriptures when its word touches our souls. Jesus
knocks softly. When one sees our modern world rushing heedlessly toward death, absorbed in its amuse-

ments, he is tempted to cry, *"Thou fool, this night thy soul shall be required of thee."* Jesus does not do this, and so we dare not. Jesus desires that we shall be conquered by His love. He says to us—and this is the glorious conclusion of our text—*If any man hear My voice and open the door, I will come in to him and will sup with him and he with Me. To him that overcometh will I grant to sit with Me in My throne, even as I also overcame and am set down with My Father in His throne.* No one can fully grasp the glory of this promise. Christ does not merely promise to share a meal with us. No, much more, we are to sit with Him upon His throne, high above the world, above death and above all satanic powers.

We have seen the danger which threatens the church that has lost its first love. We have glimpsed the riches that even such a church still possesses. Jesus still knocks. Shall we admit Him? Shall we throw back the bolt? Each of us knows the name of the particular bolt which shuts Jesus out from his life—the thing to which he holds fast even though he knows it to be contrary to the will of God.

What shall be our answer to this gracious invitation of Jesus? He does not want a rash, emotional decision. He does not force an entrance. But He continues to knock softly and *we pray in Christ's stead,* that from each of us may come that answer for which He hopes— the answer which says to Him,

> *O Lord, with shame and sorrow*
> *We open now the door;*
> *Dear Savior, enter, enter,*
> *And leave us nevermore.*

IV.
OUR MISSIONARY RESPONSIBILITY

Surely He hath borne our griefs, and carried our sorrows: ye we did esteem Him stricken, smitten of God, and afflicted. But He was wounded for our transgressions, He was bruised for our iniquities: the chastisement of our peace was upon Him; and with His stripes we are healed. All we like sheep have gone astray; we have turned everyone to his own way; and the Lord hath laid on Him the iniquity of us all. . . . He shall see of the travail of His soul, and shall be satisfied: by His knowledge shall My righteous servant justify many; for He shall bear their iniquities. Therefore will I divide Him a portion with the great, and He shall divide the spoil with the strong; because He hath poured out His soul unto death: and He was numbered with the transgressors; and He bare the sin of many, and made intercession for the transgressors.

ISAIAH 53:4-6, 11-12.

IV.

OUR MISSIONARY RESPONSIBILITY*

WHEN WE engage in the work of missions we enter a desperate spiritual struggle. We are not in a safe shelter behind the lines, but in immediate contact with the enemy. We became aware of that in Jerusalem when we observed the fanatical uprising of the Mohammedans against the Missionary Conference. All our missionaries sense the same thing as soon as they enter their field of labor. Wherever testimony to the grace of God is heard, there also, is felt the presence of the Power of Darkness. What can we do to gather quiet strength for the struggle in which we must participate? Shall we find it by considering the heroism of these young men who have obeyed the call *Get thee out of thy country, and from thy kindred, and from thy father's house, unto a land that I will show thee?* Or shall we seek it in the loyalty of our missionary societies, who receive these returning missionaries with such joy and gratitude? Both may encourage us, but they are not our ultimate source of power.

In Southern India a severe epidemic was responsible for the death of thousands living in a group of pagan villages. Only one village, a Christian one, was untouched. Then an influential non-Christian called a

* This sermon was preached at a service for newly ordained missionaries, at which a welcome was extended, also, to returning missionaries.

priestess to him and promised to build a temple to her goddess if she would transfer the plague to the Christians. A terrifying procession, led by the priestess, gathered that night and marched, amid ear-splitting shouting, to the Christian village. With her staggered a group of those who had been stricken by the plague, their faces distorted, their eyes protruding. At the same time the small company of Christians were gathered in a hut where they knelt in prayer and looked to Jesus for aid. Suddenly the awful procession stopped. "Don't you see," cried the woman, "there He stands— the God Jesus—protecting His people with outstretched hands like a shepherd protecting his lambs! He is a great God. I cannot go farther. If I did, I would die."

In this hour, when we as a missionary group confront the Power of Darkness we shall follow the example of those simple Christians in India. We will look away from everything human and fix our eyes upon the one place from which our help comes—*unto Jesus the Author and Finisher of our faith; who for the joy that was set before Him endured the cross, despising the shame.* When we Christians feel the strength of the forces arrayed against us, we can seek refuge only in Him. Says Luther, "Faith is that wherewith we attach ourselves to Christ, find reconciliation with God through Him, clothe ourselves in His person, and so live in Him that we become His own." Let us ask in this hour what it is which gives Jesus authority over the human heart. How has He conquered our hearts? And what gives Him authority over all peoples of every nation?

Often we hear it said, even upon the mission field,

that Jesus has given humanity a new and great ideal. He has founded a new social order that rests upon the principle that all men have the same rights because they are all brothers. Wherever the influence of Jesus comes, the chains of slavery fall from the negro, the power of caste is broken and the doors of prisons in which the women of the Orient are kept are thrown open. This statement contains a great truth. I shall never forget hearing a negro, whose ancestors had been slaves, address a Christian gathering in the Far East and sing, in his melodic negroid voice a song to Jesus, the Liberator. It was a great hour in the Jerusalem Conference when the women of Korea, China, Japan and India united in their testimony that Christ had restored to woman that human value which is hers as the mother of the race. But this great ideal—this new social order—which Jesus established, would never bind our hearts to Him, forever. We should look upon Him as we do Columbus, whose fearless voyages opened up a new world. But having once possessed this new world, having understood this new ideal, we should no longer need the discoverer or the founder. We erect a monument to him to show our appreciation, but we no longer need the man himself.

What is it then, that unites our hearts to Christ for all eternity? Let us seek to understand this by means of the most sacred of our human relationships. Consider the closest tie that binds us to another—the tie uniting mother and child! Why does my mother, in spite of the fact that I have outgrown some of her "old-fashioned" ideas, still exercise such a compelling power over my

heart? Not because she has formulated any great ideal.
The basis of her authority lies much deeper than that.
It rests upon the fact that, at one time she endangered
her own life to give life to me. She went close to the
gates of death that she might open to me the door of
life. That is why she possesses a unique influence upon
me and holds a permanent place in my heart. She paid
the highest price to give me existence. That she watched
at the bed of her sick child and that she sacrificed her
health for me as I grew older are but expressions of that
first great wager. Therefore, she has a claim upon me.
This human parable may perhaps point a way for us to
understand the relationship between the beginning and
the end of the fifty-third chapter of Isaiah: *Surely He
hath borne our griefs ... Therefore will I divide Him a
portion with the great, and He shall divide the spoil
with the strong.* There are things of which we seldom
speak, lest we desecrate them. The high priest passed,
but once each year, through the heavy curtain that
guarded the Holy of Holies, while in an outer court the
people waited in silent prayer. During the rest of the
year the Holy of Holies was not entered. So is it that,
only in rare hours, do we speak of the Holy of Holies of
our faith, from which we live. But in this glad moment
we may do so. With trembling hearts we approach the
hill that is surrounded with darkness because the sun
lost his splendor from the sixth to the ninth hour, during
which a desolate cry shattered the night: *My God, My
God, why hast Thou forsaken Me?* When, in spirit, we
stand at the foot of that hill, all differences between men
vanish, including the difference between the missionary

and the non-Christian to whom he is sent. For here is a word that establishes a brotherhood between us: *He bore our sorrows.*

All the differences of culture and civilization, in customs and philosophy cannot conceal the fact, that all human beings, everywhere, are afflicted by one and the same illness. That illness is estrangement from God. We all feel that if we stood close to God our relationships to other people could be arranged more satisfactorily. It is only because we are not really with God that we are enraged at every trifle. That is why those with whom we daily associate "get on our nerves." That is why the wounds which others give us do not heal. Only because he is estranged from God does the negro fall into the power of the witch-doctor and the bondage of animism. That is why the power of caste in India is not yet broken. A Chinese said to me, "We pray only to the spirits of our ancestors, for we cannot attain to the highest god. We are not pure enough for that."

But why cannot we escape from this estrangement from God that is responsible for all our ills? Because it is caused by something over which we have no power. That which separates us from God is beyond our control. It is the burden, the unforgiven debt, of our past. When one listens to an evangelist whose work lies in a European metropolis, and then to a missionary who participated in the "great revival" that swept the warlike tribes of Nias during the World war, he is amazed to note how similar are the people among whom these men work, in spite of the many contrasts in culture and customs. When, under the influence of the Holy Spirit, consciences awake and the masks, beneath which we conceal our true nature, fall away, it becomes apparent the yonder modishly dressed inhabitant of the city and the African bushman, clothed in a string of beads, are alike the bearers of secret burdens. Always the same cry breaks forth from the human heart: *When I kept silence, my bones waxed old through my roaring all the day long.* The proud Zulu in Nias falls down before the missionary, clasps his knees, tears off his heavy loincloth and permits its burden of stolen money and goods to roll on the ground. He is followed by hundreds and hundreds of others, until great heaps of gold and stolen knives and spearheads lie before the missionary. We see the same thing, although under totally different circumstances, when, in a city like Hamburg, the consciences of many who never go to church are touched and they rush into the overcrowded inquiry rooms of the evangelist. They are simply people bearing concealed burdens. It is unbelievable what is told when the sluice gates are open: abortioners, sneak-thieves, prostitutes come to confess their sin. He who must listen to such confessions for even a few hours can scarcely sleep, for his mind is filled with terrifying images.

It is these unforgiven burdens which are the weights that draw us into the bottomless depths of separation from God. We find here an awful law. The longer a sin remains unforgiven the heavier it weighs upon us, the more firmly does the Power of Darkness fasten his hold upon our soul. In every religion man has sought means to lift this burden. Great sacrifices are offered, as, for example, the great sacrifice of atonement offered on "Heaven's altar" in Peking, which is intended to reconcile Heaven and earth. The Buddhist seeks through religious exercises to shorten the long series of rebirths, through which he believes every man must pass and in which, according to the law of Karma, the consequences of all misdeeds in former existences are laid upon his shoulders, to drag him into the depths. But upon all such sacrifices and spiritual exercises rests the judgment of the *Epistle to the Hebrews: It is not possible that the blood of bulls and goats should take away sin.* We can in no way undo that which we have done.

And now into our burdened and distressed humanity comes a message as glorious as the pealing notes of a great organ or a magnificent carillon. It is a message that thrills us no matter how often it is heard. When it is proclaimed, the company of the redeemed in heaven break into psalms of praise, while countless thousands in huts of straw and in palaces, in prisons and in hospitals, who have been saved as brands from the burning, unite in prayers of thanksgiving and praise as they say, *Surely He hath borne our griefs and carried our sorrows. He was wounded for our transgressions, He was bruised for our iniquities: the chastisement of our peace was upon Him; and with His stripes we are healed.*

All the other leaders of mankind have either separated themselves from the evil of the world or have raised eloquent outcries against current vices and the lack of discipline of "modern youth." Jesus did something different from either. He assumed a totally different relationship to the world's misery and guilt. *He*

hath borne our griefs. On one occasion I watched an
Oriental porter as he prepared to take upon his back the
baggage of a group of travelers. He fastened the bun-
dles together with a strap. Around his forehead was
another strap to aid him in balancing the pack. Then
he knelt beside this mountain of luggage and, with a
single, powerful effort, placed it upon his back. His
knees quivered under the load, but he did not collapse.
As I watched him the words came to me: *He carried our
sorrows.* How the soul of Jesus trembled when He felt
the tragic burden which the Father laid upon Him! *Oh
My Father, if it be possible, let this cup pass from Me.
. . . The Lord hath laid upon Him the iniquity of us all.*
He did not evade our misery but entered into it. He
touched the lepers and ate with sinners. He bore the
burden of our transgressions to a tragic end. He would
not follow the tempting voice that said to Him, *Be it far
from Thee, Lord; this shall not be unto Thee.* The sorrow of a guilty humanity left ineffaceable traces upon
His body and soul. *He was despised and rejected of
men, a Man of sorrows and acquainted with griefs, and
we hid, as it were, our faces from Him.*

Our thinking cannot comprehend the fact that One
should take upon Himself the guilt of all. But our
conscience finds peace when, in the moment that we
realize that we cannot solve the problem of our own
life, we turn in faith to the wonderful words, *The chastisement of our peace was upon Him; and with His
stripes we are healed.* The Accuser, whose attacks
never cease, is silenced by these words. Our conscience tells us that the gigantic burden resting upon

us because of our separation from God could be lifted
only at amazing cost. It demands the most precious
thing that there is in the world. It requires the self-
surrender of the soul of the only One Who had walked
the earth in perfect purity. A mother must wager her
very life to give life to her child. In similar fashion,
the scornful word of His opponents, that contains the
entire Gospel, *must* be true of Christ: *He saved others,
Himself He cannot save.* He helped us only because
He did not help Himself, but submitted Himself to the
hate and mockery of the whole world. By doing what
no other has done He has acquired a dearly-bought
claim upon us all. *He shall divide the spoil with the
strong, because He hath poured out His soul unto death.*
That has given Him an authority over our hearts that
none can usurp. When we have once seen Him upon
the cross we can never escape Him. We may, since He
interferes with our enjoyment of life, seek to forget
Him. We may seek to undermine His claim upon us
through scientific arguments. But we have a sense of
reality that is even more basic than our intelligence and
with this deep sense of reality we must acknowledge
His claim upon us. He has impressed Himself upon us
so deeply that we can never erase Him. The missionary
labors of Paul might be described as a painting of
Christ before the eyes of men, as though He had been
crucified among you. He knew that if men could be
made to see Him as He hung upon the cross they would
be conquered. *I determined,* he said, *not to know anything among you, save Jesus Christ and Him crucified.*
John in *Revelation* tells us that an ultimate conquest of

Jesus shall come about when men shall see Him. *Every
eye shall see Him and they also which pierced Him; and
all kindreds of the earth shall wail because of Him.*

If the authority of Jesus rests upon this fact, what
follows for our task in the mission field or at home?
Our whole life shall be inadequate thanks that Christ
bore our griefs and carried our sorrows. How can we
tell this? We can win the whole world in the same way
as Christ conquered our hearts. That means that we
must permit the Crucified to change us into His image.
The most influential missionary in India asked Gandhi,
"What can we do to make Christianity native to India?"
Gandhi's head lowered thoughtfully and then he said,
"You Christians—missionaries, and all the rest—must
live like Jesus Christ; then India will not be able to
withstand you." When we view the present situation of
missions we are impressed with the fact that more and
more of the outer defences have been removed, until
the defenders have been thrown back to their central
fortress, the only place where they are invincible. The
World War and the events that are associated with it
have destroyed those things with which we previously
impressed the non-Christian world, as for example, the
possession by the so-called Christian nations of a higher
moral standard than the non-Christian peoples. What
happened in the War was that this mask of pretended
superiority was forever removed. The first defence of
Christian missions was destroyed. And now the second,
the educational program, is threatened, since the great
nations of the East have taken the work of the schools
into their own hands to use them for nationalistic pur-

poses. We still possess the third and most valuable of our outer defenses, the medical mission. But even this is no longer secure, since increasing numbers of non-Christian Oriental physicians have become skilled in Western medical knowledge.

In this development we can see the hand of God. It seems that God wishes to restrict our labors more and more, as the mountains sometimes force the Rhine into a very narrow channel. But this very limitation makes the stream deeper, swifter, more powerful. What is this narrow channel in which the stream of our labor gains depth and invincible power? It is the narrow way which the Crucified walked before us. It is the attitude which Christ assumed toward the guilt and suffering of men. Every occurrence in our community that reveals the tragic condition of man, whether it be the miserable existence of a drunkard's family or a scandal in our schools that exposes the depravity of our city's youth, reveals also two different attitudes that we can assume. On the one side stand the Pharisees who shudder with righteous indignation. On the other side are the old women of both sexes who wring their hands at the evil of this generation. Neither helps the situation in the slightest degree. There is but *one* way to heal the wounds of the world. All people, whatever philosophy they espouse, are seeking for Christ-like personalities.

The world seeks devoted men and women who do not become indignant about the world's sin, but who silently take the burden of their brothers upon their own heart. It needs men who intercede earnestly for their brethren in prayer, who are burdened with the tragedy of their fellow-men. Only along this difficult path is true influence upon others to be found. Only at this great cost can we purchase power over men. Men are not to be won through police regulations or even through noble thoughts, but only by the same method with which Christ overcame us. Paul describes the secret of his missionary success when, in the *First Epistle to the Thessalonians* he surveys his labors in that city and says, *Being affectionately desirous of you, we were willing tc have imparted unto you, not the Gospel of God only, but also our own souls, because ye were dear unto us.* Whether we have the privilege of going out as missionaries or whether our task lies at home, the "always" inadequate gratitude which we can show to Him who has healed our wounds is this, that we let His Cross shine through our lives. May our pledge be:

Thus may we serve Thee, gracious Lord!
  Thus ever Thine alone,
Our souls and bodies given to Thee,
  The purchase Thou hast won;
Through evil or through good report
  Still keeping by Thy side.
By life or death, in this poor flesh
  Let Christ be magnified!

V.

THE RETURN

A certain man had two sons: And the younger of them said, Father, give the portion of goods that falleth to me. And he divided unto them his living. And the younger son gathered all together and took his journey into a far country and there wasted his substance with riotous living. And when he had spent all, there arose a mighty famine in that land; and he began to be in want. And he went and joined himself to a citizen of that country; and he sent him into his fields to feed swine. And he would fain have filled his belly with the husks that the swine did eat: and no man gave unto him. And when he came to himself he said . . . I will arise and go to my father, and say unto him, Father, I have sinned against heaven and before thee, and am no more worthy to be called thy son. . . . But when he was yet a great way off, his father saw him, and had compassion and ran and fell on his neck and kissed him. And the son said unto him, Father, I have sinned against heaven and in thy sight, and am no more worthy to be called thy son. But the father said unto his servants, Bring forth the best robe and put it on him; and put a ring on his hand and shoes on his feet: And bring hither the fatted calf, and kill it; and let us eat and be merry. . . . Now his elder son was . . . angry, and would not go in: Therefore came his father out and entreated him. And he said to his father, Lo, these many years do I serve thee, . . . yet thou never gavest me a kid, that I might make merry with my friends: But as soon as this thy son is come, which hath devoured thy living with harlots, thou hast killed for him the fatted calf. And he said unto him, Son, thou are ever with me and all that I have is thine. It was meet that we should make merry and be glad: for this thy brother was dead and is alive again, was lost and is found.

LUKE 15:11-32.

V.

THE RETURN

THE PARABLE of the Prodigal Son was not intended originally to picture the history of every individual Jesus did not mean to suggest that everyone must fall so low. He spoke of an abnormal case which might occur under certain circumstances. He sought to emphasize that even for one who had wandered so far from the Father's house there was a path back home. Nevertheless, this story has had a remarkable effect upon those who, in succeeding ages, have heard or read it. When this story was told for the first time in a village in India, a man rushed to the missionary, crying, "Who told you that story? The man must have known *me!* It is my history!"

And everywhere that this story is heard for the first time it makes a similar impression. It is precisely because this parable portrays the greatest depth to which man can fall, that its scope includes all humanity. Each of us finds himself at some definite point in this narrative. Possibly we are already in our Father's home. We are now where we shall be throughout eternity. Nothing that may happen can drive us away from it. Perhaps we are not now enjoying our Father's peace. We are not where we should like to remain eternally, but in a strange land and among rest-

69

less companions. Then, we are either like the son of
the parable when he stormed from his home to live his
own life and to learn for himself those things against
which his pious parents had warned him, or when his
Icarus-like flight to the sun had ended in tragedy. *He
wasted his substance with riotous living.* He squandered
his possessions with harlots. The hero of liberty has
become a slave, a man who has lost his hold and fallen
into the mire of sin. Or we may have reached the third
stage: *When he had spent all, there arose a mighty
famine in that land; and he began to be in want.* His
strength is gone. The fire of enthusiasm has left only a
heap of ashes. All his beautiful dreams have vanished;
all the illusions with which he set out have collapsed.
He is like an extinct volcano. The intoxicating pleasure
has left nothing but tragic emptiness. *I perish with hunger!* Or we may have reached the fourth act of this
drama. We are then like the son as, in tattered garments, he hurries home. Day and night, across streams
and through deserts he pursues his way until he has
escaped the land where he has lost his youth and his
liberty. Here, God is being sought by a man who is no
longer an unwritten page but who has learned, all too
well, the things which the world has to offer. When we
survey these scenes which Jesus shows to us—these four
acts of the tremendous drama of humanity—we are impressed with the richness and turbulence of human life!
What long detours, over proud mountains and through
valleys of doubt, are necessary before a man can find
his way back home! But this rapidly moving picture,
that shows us the splendors of our humanly created par-

adises as well as the depths of the world's tragedy, has an immovable center that remains unchanged from the beginning to the end of the parable. That center is the fatherly heart of God, that burns with love for His child.

1. The father remains the father even though his son leaves him and, in a far country, wastes his possessions with harlots.

2. And, therefore, the father hurries toward his son when he returns home.

That is the joyful message which, by this parable, the Savior seeks to make so impressive that mankind will never forget it. Above all, it is a story which tells us that no one of us need think himself excluded from God's love.

I.

Our Father is still our Father even though we wilfully break off our relationship to Him. The Father maintains His relationship even though we live in the darkness of estrangement from Him. That is the first great truth which the parable illustrates. If a human author had written this story he would have painted this tragic farewell in brilliant colors. He would have had the father begging his son to reconsider or accusing him of rank ingratitude and saying, "Oh, you thankless boy! Think how much I have done for you! How can you leave me like this!" He would have pictured the son pulling away from the tearful embraces of his mother as she, too, seeks to restrain him. For it is this which nearly breaks the heart of parents—when a child, upon whom they have bestowed much money and effort, breaks away from his home and parental restraint to follow his own devices. But the divine character of the parable is revealed in the fact that God does not do what human parents would have done. God is greater than any human father. He does not make the slightest effort to hold back His son. *Father, give me the portion of goods that falleth to me. And he divided unto them his living.*

God does not hold back any one of us when we desire to discontinue our prayer relationship with Him. He gives us complete freedom. The autobiography of the Communist leader, Max Hoelz, tells how an overwhelming fear of being maimed came over him during the heavy artillery fire of the World War, a fear aroused by the hideous cries of the severely wounded who suffered through agonizing hours until they were released from their torment. "With the ardor of desperation I prayed for a speedy death," says Hoelz. "That was my last prayer! After those fearful hours I had no more religious illusions!" God gives us complete liberty if we thus wish to break off our relationship to Him. He places no barrier in our way. He opens the door of the parental home and says, "You may go if you wish. I will not hold you against your will." For God desires no unwilling service. He does not want a man to serve Him simply because he does not know the beauty and enchantment of the world. If there is to be a manly, free surrender there must also be the possibility of a great danger. "Youth must be wagered so that a man might be born."

God permits us to enter this world for which we

yearn. It is only through exposure to the alienating powers of the world that we can become victors. Only God can do that which no parent or teacher would dare to do. Only God can give complete liberty to a man and permit him to confront danger that may even result in his death. For God remains our Father even when we tear ourselves from Him. We live of His might even when we have tried to exclude Him from our lives. He still maintains His relationship toward us. Astronomers tell us that even when our earth, in its passage through the cold night of interstellar space, reaches its greatest distance from the sun, it is still united to it with an invisible bond. This is the gravitational pull of the sun in whose control the earth lies. It lives every moment from the power of the sun. So also is our relationship to God. Even when we lay our path through the ice-cold night of separation from God, we do not escape our dependence upon Him. *If I ascend into heaven, Thou art there; if I make my bed in hell, behold, Thou art there. If I take the wings of the morning, and dwell in the uttermost parts of the sea; even there shall Thy hand lead me, and Thy right hand shall hold me.* Even while the prodigal son squanders his money on harlots he is living from the wealth of his father. He can only destroy that which the father has given him. All our sin means, in reality, that we follow the example of the prodigal in saying to our Father, "Give me, Father, that portion of goods which is mine. I will manage my own affairs and use these possessions as pleases me."

Our sin consists in the fact that we destroy God's

gifts, and throw away the wealth which He has
given us. Our wonderfully made body is a gift of God.
It is intended to be a temple of the Holy Spirit. We
waste the glorious powers which God has implanted in
it if we destroy it through attractive poisons until only
a tragic ruin remains of the temple God has built. The
radiant eyes, which God has given us, may be misdirected to impure sights. But we can do all these things
only because the Father has given us this wealth. Even
when we doubt God, when we mock and rail at Him,
we can do so only with the mind which is His gift to us.
The power with which we sin comes from Him every
moment. We can deny God only with the capacity to
think which He gives us anew every day. For, of ourselves, we can maintain neither our body nor our spirit
for a single hour. Either could be taken from us at any
moment, in the twinkling of an eye.

II.

So our Father remains our Father even when we
withdraw ourselves from Him. He maintains His relationship even when we squander His gifts in a far
country. The Creator has never surrendered His relationship with His creation. And only because this is
true is there a possibility of return for us, just as we
are. It is the father's love that makes possible the story
of the parable. The heart of the parable lies in the
words: *But when he was yet a great way off, his father
saw him, and had compassion, and ran and fell on his
neck and kissed him.* Before any words had been
spoken, before the son could even ask for pardon, be-

fore he could show any proofs of repentance, *when he was yet a great way off, his father saw him.* Let us pause for a moment at this scene! Watch the silent embrace in which the son rests in the arms of his father, even before a word had been exchanged. The greatest artists have sought to paint this scene, but never quite successfully. And yet it becomes a reality as often as a human being, after a dreary life of doubt and sin, finds peace with God.

It was so when David, after his great sin, was received by God and cried out, *Blessed is he whose transgression is forgiven, whose sin is covered!* So it was when Saul, who had pursued the Christians with threatenings and slaughter, lay blind and helpless in his room in Damascus until Ananias laid his hand upon him with the words, *Brother Saul, the Lord, even Jesus, hath sent me, that thou mightest receive thy sight, and be filled with the Holy Ghost.* So it was when, during the "great revival" in Nias, this nation of headhunters besieged the huts of the missionaries by the hundreds, that they might confess their sins and find peace. It is always the same unbelievable miracle. The story is still: *when he was yet a great way off.* Before the confession of sin could be uttered the father ran to meet his son, fell on his neck and kissed him. *He first loved us. God commendeth His love toward us in that, while we were yet sinners, Christ died for us. When we were enemies, we were reconciled to God by the death of His Son.*

If we should have to make the first step, if we should have to begin the reconciliation with God through our tears of sorrow or through penance, we should all be lost. For we cannot repent as we ought to do. We are not able even to do that much. We are capable only of a weak and miserable attrition. Our sole salvation rests in the fact that God has made the first step. While we were still far away, the door of our Father's home was thrown open. God came through the door to become man and hurried toward us in Christ. Before we could utter a word He threw His arms around us. That is possible only because He remained our Father, even after we had sought to sever our relationship. Only because we do not come to Him, but that He instead comes to us, does the great miracle, which this parable illustrates, become possible. The son has wasted the money his father had given him. He could not restore that. He has disgraced his body. That could not be undone. Nevertheless, his father makes it possible for him to begin life over again. He prepares a banquet. He restores to his boy all the privileges of sonship. He acts toward him as though nothing had happened. The past is washed away.

Measured by every standard of human justice the protest of the elder son was entirely justified. He forms a necessary part of the parable. He but expresses that which we all feel when we hear this story. If such a thing is possible, then all the ordinances of nature and man are set at naught. It is impossible to reconcile this act with natural law. In the whole of nature there is no single violation of law that does not bring with it inevitable consequences. Nothing disappears without leaving a trace behind. The trees that have been overcome by the cold blasts of winter must stand with bare

branches in the midst of Spring's reawakening. The
most beautiful Maytime cannot recall them to life. If
through excesses we squander our youthful strength, we
lay the foundation for ailments which, with deadly certainty, will assail us as we grow older and will bring
our life to a tragic close. The inescapable laws of
heredity transfer to our children the misfortunes which
we have brought upon ourselves. In the whole of nature
there is no possibility of undoing that which has
been done.

Not only the laws of nature but also the moral law
cries out in protest. Here too the rule holds, *Whatsoever
a man soweth, that shall he also reap.* "Everyone must
eat his own soup." What would happen if there were
no retribution! The man who works hard and saves his
money will be able to provide for the necessities of his
old age. But the man who spends his time and money
solely for amusement will have cause to regret it
when he grows old. *Lo, these many years do I serve
thee,* complained the elder brother, *neither transgressed
I at any time thy commandment: and yet thou never
gavest me a kid that I might make merry with my
friends; but as soon as this thy son was come, which
hath devoured thy living with harlots, thou hast killed
for him thy fatted calf!* The elder brother might perhaps have had no objection if the prodigal, since he
acknowledged his wrongdoing, had been received into
the household, not as a son—he had not earned that—
but as a hired servant. The prodigal himself had not
expected more than this. His brother felt that he should
be treated in such a way that he would never forget the

injury which he had done his father. He should not be allowed to gain any higher position. That is how we humans would do things. This would be in harmony with natural law. It would be in keeping with the moral order of the world which demands that a man must reap the things he has sown. If another has stolen from us and has deceived us and then asks our forgiveness, we are perhaps willing to take his hand and say, "I am willing to associate with you once more." But still it will always remain a tarnished friendship. We cannot forget that which he has done.

But how does God act? *The father said to his servants, Bring forth the best robe, and put it on him; and put a ring on his hand, and shoes on his feet; and bring hither the fatted calf, and kill it; and let us eat, and be merry; for this my son was dead, and is alive again; he was lost and is found.* The whole house was prepared for the feast. The music and the sound of dancing could be heard far across the fields. The calf, which had been fattened for some noteworthy occasion, was slain. The prodigal son is restored to all the dignity of sonship and is given the privilege of starting life anew. That is how God acts. That is the miracle of forgiveness. That is how He treated Paul, the chief of sinners, who had persecuted the church of God. Had the decision been placed in the hands of other apostles they would, no doubt, since he realized his errors, have received him as a member of the Christian community. There he would have been observed as to his conduct and attitude. He would have been placed on probation. But God lifted this persecutor from the dust to the highest

place without any transitional pauses. He was forgiven
everything. God said, *He is a chosen vessel unto me.*
This is the miracle of forgiveness. Only God can do
this. For only God can set aside the ordinances of
nature and life.

This is the glorious possibility which God offers us.
No matter how our life has been wasted and corrupted
there is still a possibility that we may begin once more
from its beginning. Each of us, even though his back
is bowed under seven decades of life with all its burdens, sins, and disappointments, can this very day begin
his life once more. For the Father Who came to meet
us when we were still far away, is Master of the natural
law of retribution. That which makes us old is not the
decreasing powers of our body. It is a gracious thing
that we are not forced to live eternally. Becoming old is
not an external but an internal occurrence. We become
old because of the memories that have left deep marks
upon our inner life, the scars of wounds which continue
to burn, because of the many things in our life of which
we say, "What would I not give if I could do, or undo,
that again!"

It is these which make us old and fretful and bitter
and weary of life. And now God offers to remove all
these burdens from us. We are to become like the prodigal son in the moment when he sat beside his father at
the banquet table, overwhelmed by so great a love which
wiped out the whole of his tragic past. When those
things which make us old fall from our shoulders we are
born again and become like the children. Then we can
recommence our relationships in home and business.

Our life will become as beautiful as on the morning of creation. In the *Book of Micah* we read, *Thou wilt cast all their sins into the depths of the sea.* When an ocean liner sails in mid-ocean, the sailors throw overboard a great mass of useless objects, broken tools, garbage and dirt. If this were done on some shallow lake the water would be contaminated. But the ocean is so deep that no traces are left. A few seconds after these things are throw overboard, the bluish gray water is clear and undisturbed as before. No one can draw forth that which has been cast into the ocean. It has sunk into the wellnigh fathomless depths. And so God says to us, *I cast all your sins into the depths of the sea.*

Why have we not all accepted this miraculous offer long ago? It is accompanied by a condition which is entirely reasonable but which, nevertheless, prevents many from accepting it. The prodigal son could only fall silently into his father's arms. He could give no proofs that his repentance is sincere, that he would henceforth be a different person and that he was not driven home simply by poverty and hunger. He could bring but one thing with him. That was the knowledge: *I am no more worthy to be called thy son.* He was conscious of the fact that he was utterly worthless. And he also knew that his father knew this of him. If his father should still receive him it would not be because the son had anything of value to offer. From that moment the son must be entirely dependent upon the mercy of his father. He knew, "I have lost my own dignity. My entire existence must now depend upon my father's goodness."

The simple and wholly reasonable condition of our entrance into the new life is this same acknowledgment. But, though it is very simple, it is, nevertheless, extremely difficult for the natural man to do. We do not want to surrender our own dignity. We do not want to be beggars and live upon charity. The prodigal son determined to build his new life entirely upon the mercy of his father. Not even the attitude of his elder brother could drive him away. But we do not want to live by grace. Even when some person that we much admire offers us his friendship, we want to feel that we can contribute something to this relationship. Even when we are poverty stricken, within and without, we are careful to conceal the fact. We do not want to stand as a beggar before him and receive the free gifts of his love. That offends our self respect. We desire that he should value us for what we have to offer. But, with regard to God, we find ourselves in a very painful situation. We cannot pretend before Him. He knows us through and through. He knows that we are worthless. Nevertheless, He wants to give us another chance. The single, reasonable condition of entrance into our Father's house is that we acknowledge our true condition and build our new life entirely upon this knowledge.

Shortly before his last illness, Ludwig Hefacker, that Swabian man of God, wrote, "What shall I bring when I come to Thee, my Savior? Acts of self-denial, spiritual struggles, prayers, faithfulness, love, faith? No, I can bring nothing to Thee. If Thou should look upon me in grace, I shall be saved. But if Thou should look upon me in the disfavor I have a million times deserved, I must enter eternal darkness. But Thou art love and unending mercy." That remained his soul's anchor until his end. It may also be that for us.

We have considered the history of man and the center about which this history moves, the heart of the Father that burns with love even though we turn from Him in wilful pride and that hurries to meet us when we have taken but a single returning step. May this awaken in all of us the burning wish to say, *I will arise and go to my Father!*

VI.

THE TWO WAYS OF MAN

I speak after the manner of men, because of the infirmity of your flesh: for as ye have yielded your members servants to uncleanness and to iniquity unto iniquity; even so now yield your members servants to righteousness unto holiness. For when ye were the servants of sin, ye were free from righteousness. What fruit had ye then in those things whereof ye are now ashamed? for the end of those things is death. But now being made free from sin, and become servants to God, ye have your fruit unto holiness and the end everlasting life. For the wages of sin is death; but the gift of God is eternal life through Jesus Christ our Lord.

ROMANS 6: 19-23

VI.

THE TWO WAYS OF MAN

IN THE Campo Santo in Pisa, one of the loveliest cemeteries of Italy, there is to be seen a beautiful piece of statuary, "The Triumphal March of Death." It depicts a procession of knights in full armor laughing gaily among themselves, until they are halted abruptly by three open caskets, from which skeletons grin at the riders. This summarizes the conflict in which humanity lives. One may be made especially conscious of it on some holiday occasion or other. There go a youthful group of merrymakers through the streets. Suddenly their song is silenced as a funeral procession passes. Again: in a metropolitan tenement, in which the families are all strangers to one another, there may be dancing on one floor, while directly overhead a man lies at death's door. Through the windows that are thrown open to give relief to the fever-stricken sufferer comes the tinkle of glasses and the laughter of carefree youth. That is the sort of contrast in which humanity lives. On the one side festivity with waving flags, wreaths of flowers and carefree pleasantries, on the other, a picture, such as no newspaper reader can forget, of Malmgreen dying alone on the icefields, while his companions press on without him. This is the contrast between the two worlds in which we live, the contrast between smiling life and tragic death. Our entire fate as human beings is summed up in such a contrast.

All our poets, artists and philosophers have attempted to cast some revealing light upon this conflict of our existence. Death, they say, comes as a friend to release us from the bondage of time. It frees us from the dungeon of the flesh. The soul is a bird which spreads its wings when the cage is opened, and flies into the blue heavens. Death is merely a homecoming—an entrance to a higher and eternal existence in which we are lost, like a drop of water in a trackless sea.

Those of us who can find satisfaction in such explanations of death are not among those for whom this chapter in *Romans* was written. But one who has stood at the deathbed of a relative, and looked upon the grey reality of death, or who has witnessed the futile struggle of a young man as he clings to life with every atom of his departing strength, can never be satisfied with any of these attempted explanations of death. What does this Scripture passage say to us? It tells us of an unbridged chasm, an irreconcilable contrast between life and death. For this contrast is rooted in the ultimate implacable contrast between God and sin. *The wages of sin is death; but the gift of God is eternal life through Jesus Christ our Lord!*

We stand between two worlds, or rather, between two forces which seek our allegiance. Every day we confront an Either-Or which compels a decision from us. Let us, in the light of our text, place clearly before our eyes the irreconcilable contrast between these two worlds:

1. The Power of Darkness, which leads us into slavery and whose end is death;

2. The triumphant power of Jesus, which leads us into liberty and whose end is eternal life.

I.

The wages of sin is death. Is that really true? Is sin really so dreadful and so dangerous? Is this statement not an exaggeration? If one tells a "white lie" or spends a night in drunken carousal with some friends, is any great harm done? "No one who walks the dusty ways of this life can come to the end of his journey without having dirtied his clothes and without having fallen to the ground at one time or another. Everyone, even the best of men, is guilty of some youthful prank." That is how people talk when they speak of sin. And they are entirely right if sin is nothing more than dust and dirt which we can brush from our clothes. If such were the case our sins would be harmless enough. But here is a word which takes fundamental issue with this superficial view of sin: *Ye have yielded your members to uncleanness* and then *ye were the slaves of sin*. (For that is the literal translation of Paul's words). We are, then, not dealing with single violations of laws, with mere boyish pranks. Behind these single actions stands a Power that has but one purpose, which utilizes every means to rob us of our most precious possession, our freedom, our lordship over ourselves.

It is a tragic truth that *Whosoever committeth sin is the slave of sin.* So long as the deed is not yet done, so long as the angry word is not yet spoken, so long as the letter in which we lie our way out of a difficulty is not

yet written, so long as we have not yet surrendered to
an impure passion, we are still free. But as soon as
the deed is done, it is as though a prison door which we
can never open has closed upon us. In the dark days
when slave hunters went from village to village in
Africa, the frightened native fled deep into the jungle,
but his pitiful flight was ended when a hunter could
throw a lasso over his head. Then there was no possibility of escape. He was taken to the camp where he
was chained to other slaves and forced, by the leather
whips of the guards, to cross the burning deserts to the
coast. There he was chained in the hold of the ship and
carried to a foreign land where he spent the rest of his
life in miserable slavery.

That illustration may visualize for us the tragic relationship that is meant by the words, *Ye have yielded
your members to uncleanness, and to iniquity unto iniquity*. Perhaps it was only a simple lie told to provide
an easy escape from an unpleasant situation, or an act
which a young man committed while under the influence of liquor that cast a lasso over his head. If this
lasso is not immediately destroyed through the power
of God, then he is drawn from iniquity to iniquity.
For there is a Power at work which is not concerned
with little things, but which gambles for larger stakes.
He has but one concern. By one means or another he
seeks to bring us under his power. He takes advantage
of our weak points, for he knows that if we surrender
our liberty at one place we are altogether lost. There is
no stopping then. Consider David. He cast an impure
glance at a woman; then he was drawn into a treacher-

ous resolve to do away with the man who stood in his way, a resolve which ended in a cowardly murder. That happened to a man who had enjoyed fellowship with God. From one impurity we are drawn to increasingly greater offenses, because our freedom has been lost.

I was once an observer at the court-martial of an officer who had previously been awarded the Iron Cross for distinguished bravery. He was accused of having stolen some money, like a common pickpocket. It was difficult to understand how a hero could do such a thing. But his trial brought out the fact that he had, at one time, been given morphine to ease the pain of the wounds from which he suffered. By the time this had been repeated three or four times, he had been brought under the power of the drug and had become an addict, a slave of narcotics. Then he needed money to buy the morphine for which he craved. So, step by step, he went down the path which led to common thievery. When we have once given our members into slavery they become increasingly enslaved. One member after another becomes bound by the chains. The eyes become impure. No longer can we look at a member of the other sex with pure eyes. Conscience becomes stilled, and the ears of the soul deaf to the voice of God.

Every man who, for the first time, sins against the commandment of purity experiences a sense of burning shame. But after the second and third violation, his conscience is dumb. Every child is ashamed when, for the first time, it tells a lie. It can hardly believe that it has done this dreadful thing. But after a few times the voice of the conscience is no longer heard. The

Prince of Darkness is like the slave hunter. When once
he has an unfortunate individual in his power, he forces
him to do his will. His victims are chained together
with other slaves. It is worthy of note that a slave of
evil immediately finds companions with whom he can
associate. They mutually lead one another to destruction. This makes the Power against whom we fight
even more terrible. Behind these little temptations
lurks this dreadful Power whose sole purpose it is to
rob us of our liberty, that gift of God without which we
cannot live. It may be that harmless things are used to
gain this end. The glass of beer which gradually becomes indispensable, a dose of morphine that the doc-
tor prescribes too often or a package of cigarettes to
which a man becomes so accustomed that he cannot
work without them—all these are weapons in the hand
of the Destroyer. Behind these innocent things stands
a Power that is not interested in unimportant things,
but which seeks to fasten its chains upon us. The
Power which seeks to destroy us is like a great python
which slowly enfolds its victim, as with a loving embrace. But when its victim has come into its power the
embrace becomes tighter, until finally, when the entire
body of its prey has been enveloped, its life is choked
out of it.

Now we may understand something of the meaning
of the words: *What fruit had ye then in those things
whereof ye are now ashamed? For the end of those
things is death. . . For the wages of sin is death.*

Why is death the end of the way along which sin
leads us? What is the relationship between them? What

have they to do with one another, this physical dying, which is, after all, only a collapse of our bodies, and that evil of which our consciences accuse us? Are they not two entirely different things? Many have, in the course of illness, become aware of this dark relationship. If their conscience could have been freed from the guilt of a lie, their body would have been well. The relationship between body and conscience is a very close one. Why do we shudder so before death, even the bravest of us, who fear no bodily pain? The collapse of the body is not the most difficult thing to bear in death. Rather it is the fact that our soul must enter this dark tunnel. Everything in us rebels against it. The last remnant of our liberty is taken from us. We find ourselves in the grip of a Power which drags us down, even as a swimmer who is caught in a dangerous eddy is dragged down. In both instances it is a power which seeks to destroy us and to rob us of the last remnant of our freedom. *The sting of death,* says Paul, *is sin . . . The wages of sin is death.* The Might, which has separated us from God, here pays us our wages. In death we must once more deal with that Power which would wrest us from God and drag us into the abyss of separation from Him. Its last attempt to claim us is made here.

II.

Only after we have, with sober insight, seen the tragic relationship between the slavery of sin and death, are we filled with jubilant thanksgiving when we hear the message: *The wages of sin is death; but the gift of*

God is eternal life through Jesus Christ our Lord. There is, then, not only a way of slavery which leads to death; there is also a way of freedom which leads to life. Paul draws our attention to a noteworthy agreement between these two contrary paths *As ye have yielded your members servants to uncleanness and to iniquity unto iniquity; even so now yield your members servants to righteousness unto holiness.* We saw that behind all the small enticements and temptations of life stands a great Power which seeks only to enchain us. In the same way, behind all the invitations of the Gospel which we have heard from childhood, behind the prayers of our mother and the earnest advice of Christian friends, behind all these stands another Power, the Conqueror of death, the Prince of Easter, who has redeemed us from the slavery of death. He seeks to win us. He also has but one purpose, to free us from the slavery of death. That is the goal of His labor for us. That is why He said to the rich young ruler, *Sell that thou hast and give to the poor.* He wished to free him from the chains of his wealth. That is why He said to the malefactor, *Today shalt thou be with Me in paradise.* Even at the last moment Christ wished to release him from the slavery of a misdirected life. He seeks all of us that He may give us that indescribable gift which enables us to return to the condition in which we came from God's hand.

There is a notable agreement between the way of slavery and the way of freedom and life: in both cases the first step is of supreme importance, for it determines all future strides. There is a first step that enables the Prince of Darkness to throw his lasso over our heads, so that he can lead us to the bitter end. So, also, there is a first step toward liberty which has blessed consequences: *Yield your members servants to righteousness.* What does that mean? Paul says, *I speak after the manner of men,* for he knows that he must express himself so simply that everyone can understand him. He does not say that we are to accept a new philosophy of life, that our thoughts are to find a new direction. Possibly a few of us would have understood him better had he said that. But he says very simply: *Yield your members servants to righteousness.* Liberty does not depend upon grandiose ideas, but upon the conservation of our members. That is where freedom begins. The result of this war of emancipation in which we take part depends upon our eyes, that we determine not to look upon certain things with them; upon our ears, that we again learn to hear God's words; upon our mouth, that the tongue be freed from backbiting and slander that it may glorify God.

In this way the members of our body must be dedicated to God. Our surrender begins with our members. The Enemy seizes us at *one* point that he might rob us of our liberty. And so redemption begins also at *one* point in our nature, from which everything else is to be changed. Our tongue must be set free. Our mouth must be willing to make a frank confession, that should long since have been held, in order that a network of lies might be destroyed. As soon as we begin with one such simple and practical matter, we become aware that the air of freedom streams in at this point. We have come into contact with the resurrection power of the

Savior, with the fulness of life that He brought. When one bond has been broken and one member set free for God, we are surrounded by the fresh air of morning. Our newly-found freedom soon reaches over into other spheres. We receive new eyes, eyes that are pure and that look upon God's creation with gratitude and joy. We are given a new ear that is attentive unto the voice of God. Sin placed us in a caravan of slaves, a fellowship of prisoners. Now, when we have yielded our members to the service of Christ and have at one point carried out the surrender of which Paul speaks, we are received into a new fellowship, into a fellowship of free men. We are drawn to others who have the same liberty, no matter to what class of society or to what race they belong. There is an army of fighters for the light from all peoples and from all conditions of men. They understand one another immediately when they meet, even though they have never seen one another before. They are united by strong inner ties.

And the end of this way of freedom is eternal life. *But now being made free from sin and become servants to God, ye have your fruit unto holiness, and the end everlasting life.* All of us, even though we have our liberty, must pay tribute to death. It will be difficult, but we must pass through the same dark stream. We must once more come into contact with that dark Power that wills our destruction. We could never survive this contact by virtue of our own strength. We are not equal to the impact of his attack. For the whole burden of our guilt draws us downward. But when we have been set free through Christ, we pass through safely. We read in the New Testament that we have eternal life in Christ Jesus our Lord. I once watched a great fire in which the flames had reached the third floor of the building. A gray-haired fireman climbed up a towering ladder and reached into a window of the third story, where the streams of water were hissing against the flames, to rescue a child. He held it secure in his arms and with sure grip climbed down the ladder to safety. The child looked fearfully about, but still rested securely in the arms of its rescuer.

So it is with the death of a liberated man. We are not spared the horror of death. We shall feel the flames through which we are being carried. The streams of water will hiss about us. In fact, Christians have often come very near losing their faith in the presence of death. They had nothing to sustain them in that moment. We dare not take death lightly. But we have One in Whose arms we may rest and Who bears us safely through fire and water. At the moment of death it would not be enough if He were only to go before us as an example. We must stand much closer to Him than that. It must be true what Luther said, "Christian faith is that through which we cling to Christ, pay God with Him, clothe ourselves with His person, yes, lose ourselves entirely in His love, and be His own!" When we are bound to Him like that, we will come through the ordeal of death, by which the Prince of Darkness seeks to destroy us, to life.

We have seen the two ways between which we must choose, the way into which the Power of Darkness would draw us and whose end is death, and the way of deliverance whose end is life.

To which of these powers shall we belong? We cannot follow both at the same time. Either we are earning the wages of death or else we are rejoicing in the life which is given us by our Deliverer.

May this be the solemn pledge of every one:

> *Lord, Thou fount of joy forever,*
> *Thou art mine,*
> *I am Thine,*
> *No one can us sever.*

> *I am Thine, because Thou gavest*
> *Life and blood*
> *For my good.*
> *By Thy death me savest.*

> *Thou art mine, I love and own Thee;*
> *Ne'er shall I,*
> *Light of joy,*
> *From my heart dethrone Thee.*

> *Let me, let me soon behold Thee,*
> *Face to face,*
> *Thy embrace—*
> *May it soon enfold me!*

PAUL GERHARDT.
Tr. J. KELLY.

VII.

WORDS—HUMAN AND DIVINE

For ye remember, brethren, our labor and travail: for labor-
ing night and day, because we would not be chargeable unto
any of you, we preached unto you the Gospel of God. Ye are
witnesses, and God also, how holily and justly and unblame-
ably we behaved ourselves among you that believe: as ye know
how we exhorted, and comforted, and charged every one of
you, as a father doth his children, that ye would walk worthy
of God, who hath called you into His kingdom and glory. For
this cause also thank we God without ceasing, because, when
ye received the Word of God which ye heard of us, ye received
is not as the word of men, but as it is in truth, the Word of
God, which effectually worketh also in you that believe.

I Thessalonians 2: 9-13

VII.

WORDS—HUMAN AND DIVINE

THIS TEXT transports us into the midst of a great event, the entrance of the Christian Gospel into pagan Europe. It takes us to the beginning of that spiritual struggle which resulted in the complete transformation of that continent. The very first entrance of Christian faith into Europe aroused the bitter antagonism with which the Western World has always met Christ. That which occurred in the Macedonian cities of Philippi and Thessalonica was but a foretaste of the struggle, which would continue even to our own day upon European soil, between Christ and Antichrist. The converted jailor in Philippi had washed the wounds of Paul and Silas which he had himself inflicted the day before. Then, their backs still covered with gashes, they had traveled the next day to Thessalonica, that they might seek to conquer this second fortress for Christ. But scarcely had they arrived, when a boisterous crowd assailed the house in which they had found shelter, crying, *These, that have turned the world upside down, are come hither also!* Why should these two men, who entered the city without financial or military support and who possessed little beside their wounds, call forth such angry excitement that great crowds regarded them as dangerous to the peace of the whole world? Why is it that the Russian Communists take such strong action to silence those few simple men who travel from village to village as messengers of the Gospel? Why are they not simply ridiculed as "old-fashioned emotionalists" and defenders of an "exploded superstition"?

The reason for this antagonism is stated in the words with which Paul summarizes his picture of those great events: *For this cause also we thank God without ceasing, because, when ye received the Word of God which ye heard of us, ye received it not as the word of men, but as it is in truth, the Word of God.* These very simple words describe the wonderful event which, wherever and whenever it occurs, touches the depths of men's hearts and, on the one hand, brings into being a movement in which men dedicate themselves to God even at the cost of life, and, on the other hand, a group of those who reject it vigorously even to the point of shedding blood. It is the same experience which is seen repeatedly on all mission fields and upon which the whole church rests. It is an event for which Paul thanks God without ceasing.

What is the nature of this strange event? While the Apostle testified to the Savior of sinners in weak human words, a change took place with these words when they were received into the hearts of the hearers. They were received, no longer as mere human words, but as the Word of God. Thus the most impotent thing upon the earth, the human word of the sermon, is transformed into the mightiest thing which there is, the Word of God, *which effectually worketh in you that believe,* a Word, that is, which bears within it the whole power of God.

18707

Let us consider this miracle which the Holy Spirit per-
forms and through which God's people are constantly
reborn; the miracle which we can experience new every
day when we read the Bible prayerfully—that of a
merely human word wonderfully changed into a Word
of God, which contains the power and permanence of
eternity.

I.

That which the Apostle said was a human word is,
clearly, a reference to the word of his sermons—the
missionary testimony which he and Silas sought, with
simple insistence, to bring to the Thessalonians. It
was the message that Jesus was the Christ. It was
not a thunderous voice from heaven. Neither was
it a speech from which the last vestige of the human
spirit was erased. In former days men believed that
when God spoke through men, it was necessary that the
human spirit of the speaker be completely silenced. It
was thought that the sacred writers, like Moses or
Isaiah, were entirely unconscious when they received
their revelations. For when God spoke, man could be
nothing more than an otherwise inanimate instrument,
upon which God played. But such was not the case. In
our text Paul speaks of words that were spoken by the
clear consciousness of the speaker. They were simple
human words, through which the apostles sought to convince Thessalonica of the truth of the Gospel which they
brought.

Is there anything more impotent than a human
word? We may observe it again as we follow the de-

liberations concerning disarmament. Of what value are
words that are not backed by military power by which
force can be exercised! What a pitiful sight it is when
on the one side there are only words, only impotent
protests, while on the other are cannon, battleships and
millions of men armed to the teeth! But when words
in general are so weak, how feeble and subject to criticism are merely human words concerning matters of
faith, the words of a sermon! A few years ago in Berlin
a questionnaire was sent to thousands of people. One of
the questions was, "What do you think of the value of
sermons?" A shoemaker wrote, "The sermon is stupe-
fying. I consider the Bible a rank falsehood." A teacher
answered, "The sermon is a jumble of meaningless
phrases. People who think for themselves can receive
no help from it. The same is true of liturgy." It is easy
to understand the reason for such opinions. For of what
value is a human word concerning the question of eternity if it is only the word of a man? What help can it
give us, if another finite person tells us his unauthori-
tative opinions concerning eternal realities? Our human
opinions seldom stand for more than a few decades, at
longest. We are confused as we listen to a wealth of
contradictory views. Every voice has something different to say. Whom shall we believe? It becomes increasingly difficult to find one's way through the labyrinth
of human philosophy! How can it help us, who, in approaching death, are approaching also another world
which lies beyond our horizon, if another man voice his
opinion, even though he express it in the deep tones of
sacred conviction? He who speaks to us has but a lim-

ited horizon, even as you and I. His view does not reach beyond that which we ourselves can see and touch.

But it is not merely by reason of its being spoken by limited, time-bound preachers, that a human word concerning human problems is so impotent. It is due, in far greater measure, to the fact that it is uttered by sinful men. It is this fact which so often robs the sermons, preached in our churches, of their power. Just as a truck, too heavily loaded, finds it impossible to climb a hill, so is the word, which the church speaks concerning God, overburdened by the sinfulness of those who declare it, rendered pointless and ineffectual. The words are robbed of power because they are spoken by sinners. It is not possible to entirely separate a message from the one who presents and advocates it. How frequently, today, we hear the cry, which the Stoics and Epicureans raised against Paul in Athens, *"What will this babbler say?* This fellow cannot impress us very much! Surely he does not expect us to take *him* seriously."* That is why there are few things which make a weaker impression than the Gospel of the Crucified, the very human word of the sermon. Many things in the life of today are so much stronger: military power, for example, that is strong enough to destroy all opposition; the alluring pleasures of art, that enable us to forget ourselves and which make their appeal to our attention through flaming advertisements and shrieking billboards.

II.

Is there anything more impotent than the human

word of the sermon? But now God does something which staggers our imagination—something for which Paul will thank Him throughout all eternity. This most impotent thing that the world knows is taken by God and transformed into the most powerful thing there is in it. The human words which the Apostle spoke in Thessalonica and which he wrote in the Epistles that we today read, is received, *not as the word of men, but as it is in truth, the word of God.* Here we stand before the mystery of God's methods. *God hath chosen the weak things of the world to confound the things which are mighty . . . It pleased God by the foolishness of preaching to save them that believe.* With majestic freedom God ignores all the powers of earth and selects that which is weakest and most defenseless, the human word of the sermon, subjected as it is to the criticism of the world, and lays in it His divine power, power which conquers all the forces of hell. There is nothing remarkable in the copper wires we can see as we drive through the country. They appear to be no different from any other strong wires. They can scarcely be distinguish from wire used to fence pastures. Yet these are high tension wires, which carry an invisible load of gigantic power. In touching them the strongest man would be hurled to the ground. They supply an entire city with light and power. They stretch from a far distant waterfall, and carry the energy of its tumbling, rushing waters. So the unassuming word of the Apostle looks, at first glance, like any other human word, such as one man may speak to another. Yet it is charged with a power that can hurl the strongest to the ground;

it contains the energy which emanates from the distant, rushing waters of eternity.

While in the garden of Alypius, Augustine heard a voice chanting the words, "Take up and read; take up and read." Seizing the volume of the Epistles of the Apostle Paul, he read, *Not in rioting and drunkenness, not in chambering and wantonness, not in strife and envying; but put ye on the Lord Jesus Christ, and make not provision for the flesh.* "No further would I read," wrote he in his *Confessions,* "nor needed I: for, instantly, at the end of this sentence, by a light as it were of serenity infused into my heart, all the darkness of doubt vanished away." A single word of the New Testament was the means by which God removed the chains from this man and took away the blindness of his eyes. This single word of the Bible gave a leader to the church during the whole period of the Middle Ages. A single verse in the first chapter of *Romans* freed Luther and became for him "the gate to paradise." This single verse of the New Testament was responsible for a transformation of much of the world's history. How are these things possible? Only because God is present through His Spirit in this Word. While we sit bowed over our Bibles and while our eyes read the printed words, it may happen to us as happened, long ago, to the servant of Elisha, after the prophet had prayed, *Lord, I pray Thee, open his eyes that he may see. And the Lord opened the eyes of the young man, and he saw: and, behold, the mountain was full of horses and chariots of fire round about Elisha.* While we listen with our physical ears to this word, another ear is opened through the power of the Holy Spirit; the ear for God that, possibly, has been deaf for a long, long time; the ear of which our Lord spoke so often when he said, *He that hath ears to hear, let him hear!*

But if we stand before God, if He truly speaks with us, then nothing else really matters. Then the human being who speaks this word to us becomes suddenly quite unimportant and subsidiary, for we are alone with God, even as Moses on Sinai was alone with God. If God is here, then everything which God gives and has is here also: the power of God over those forces which assault us on every hand, His power which frees us from the burden of our conscience, His power to give us a new heart and a new spirit. It is true, as Luther says, "We enter another school, in which the Holy Spirit is the teacher, and He writes these words, not with pen and ink, but with fiery flames upon our hearts." And Melanchthon adds the thought, "Study alone does not enable us to understand the sacred Scriptures, but it is necessary that, with the Holy Spirit as our Instructor, we experience their power in the changing circumstances of life." If God instructs us through His Holy Spirit, then He is present with all His power in His Word, even when we feel nothing of it. *The Word of God, which effectually* WORKETH *also in you that believe.* God cannot be inactive. We feel His power over the forces of darkness which attack us. He is there with His power to reconcile our consciences to Himself.

The more mature we become as Christians, the

clearer it becomes to us that we cannot continue to live upon the experiences of the past. The last refuge of our inner life, the ultimate source of our peace and our courage in the face of disaster, is the Word of promise. It is the anchor of our soul and the only inexhaustible fountain of strength. In our younger years—in the springtime of life—we may be supported by a wave of enthusiasm. But when we have learned to know the other side of life; when the flames of enthusiasm have died down leaving only a heap of rapidly cooling embers; when winter storms have torn the leaves from the tree of our life, we learn that temptation can be overcome only through the Word. *Unless Thy Word had been my comfort, I should have perished in mine affliction.* (Ps. 119:92, Luther's Translation) And finally, in the struggle of death, when there is no strength left in us upon which we can draw; when the powers of our soul are withered and the Accuser attacks us day and night—the Word becomes greater and more precious than ever before. We cling to the Word, as Luther told us, like a man, slipping down a cliff, clings to a rope that is thrown to him and which alone can save him from the depths below. We cling fast to its great promises, and read over and over again, *Fear not, for I have redeemed thee. I have called thee by thy name; thou art Mine.* We find refuge in the words of Jesus, *He that cometh to Me I will in no wise cast out.* We can have no other resting place. Even our prayers find their expression more and more in the words of the Psalms. We understand Luther's meaning, when he says, "The Word itself must satisfy our hearts, without any other authority. It alone must thoroughly convince us, so that we are imprisoned by it, even though all the world, the very angels or all the princes of hell should say otherwise— yea, even if God himself should test His elect and seem to say something else than He has already said." When we read the promises of Scripture to a dying man, we become aware that the whole power of Jesus' death lies in them, that a single word is strong enough to sustain a helpless person above water for a whole night. Faith is nothing else than that movement which we must always make, away from ourselves and from our own feelings and variable moods, to the Word.

If all this is true, then every contact with the Word, whether we listen to it in the church or read it at home, is of immeasurable importance. If it were only a human word—an address in which a man describes his experiences or expresses his ideas of life's meaning— then it would be a harmless business to listen to it for a time. We can do so for entertainment or to "fill in" until we have something of more importance to do. But we cannot come into contact with God or His Word without endangering our entire life. When God speaks with us, we stand before our Judge, Who knows all about us. Near the high tension wires, which carry powerful electric currents, we see signs bearing the words, "Danger! Keep away!" So contact with this Word, through which flows the power of God, is also dangerous. *For our God is a consuming fire.* We cannot come in contact with the Word without becoming conscious immediately of the chains which encircle us. If we continue to associate with the Word and yet do not break these bonds, we should be far better off if we join ourselves to an atheist association and forget all about worship and the church. Otherwise, we shall only continue to harden our hearts. That is why Paul reminds us that he preached the Gospel of God *in fear and in much trembling.* He strained every nerve to bring his hearers into contact with the greatest thing in life. He brought his message and personal counsel to every individual he could reach. *For ye remember, brethren, our labor and travail: for laboring night and day, because we would not be chargeable unto any of you, we preached unto you the Gospel of God. Ye are witnesses, and God also, how holily and justly and unblameably we behaved ourselves among you that believe.* He knew how dangerous it is for a man to receive the Word, if his life is not thereby changed. *As ye know how we exhorted and comforted and charged every one of you, as a father doth his children, that ye walk worthy of God, Who hath called you into His kingdom and glory.* The same is true of the work of every sincere pastor in a modern congregation. Contact with the Word of God is still the most glorious and the most dangerous act in life.

We have spoken of the miracle to which the church of God owes its existence, the miracle by which God infuses all the power of eternity into human words, which, of themselves, are among the most impotent things in all the world. That God still speaks to us today is something that lies beyond our control. And yet we can live only because He does. Dostoievsky has said, "A people without God cannot endure, for its soul thirsts for the Word of God." May God never remove from us the might of His Word!

VIII.

AN IMPERISHABLE CROWN

Know ye not that they which run in a race run all, but one receiveth the prize? So run, that ye may attain. And every man that striveth for the mastery is temperate in all things. Now they do it to obtain a corruptible crown: but we an incorruptible I therefore so run, not as uncertainty; so fight I, not as one that beateth the air; but I keep under my body, and bring it into subjection: lest that by any means, when I have preached to others, I myself should be a castaway.

I CORINTHIANS 9: 24-27

VIII.

AN IMPERISHABLE CROWN

IT IS a well known fact, attested to by physicians, that many men who, before the World War suffered from various nervous diseases and had become burdens to their families or were inmates in suitable institutions, were suddenly restored to health at the outbreak of hostilities. What was the cause of this? Until then, their lives had been self-centered. But then something entered into their lives which took possession of them from morning till night and which caused themselves to forget themselves and their misfortunes. And so, as soldiers confronted with the threat of death, they become healthy individuals. This fact reveals what is really the deepest need of men. It is not an infirm body, or lack of money, or the absence of many advantages which others possess, that constitutes our greatest need. The deepest misery is that which a man has when his life possesses no ultimate purpose, when he has nothing to take him beyond himself. A man who knows of no pearl so costly that he would gladly sell all others to gain it, is a miserable man. There are many such people today. That is the fundamental ailment of our generation.

We have, in our day, accomplished great things in many different fields of activity. Nevertheless, there are thousands who have not achieved genuine and thankful joy in life because they have seen no other goal before them than a week of labor, a week-end of lethargy and then another round on the treadmill of life. What does it all mean? What purpose does it all have? To these questions there is no answer. That is why the number of neurotics increases daily and the number of suicides rises to such tragic heights. One does not turn open the gas-jets merely because his wages are insufficient to provide for his needs or because of unrequited love. There is a more basic cause. It is the nothingness —the darkness of futility—that seems to stand behind all of life. If we read the words of the Apostle which form our text with eyes open to the need of our day, we shall be impressed with the glory of them. At first reading, they seem to be a series of difficult dramas, of whip lashes that drive us forward unmercifully: *So run, that ye may attain! . . . I keep under my body!* But when we penetrate a bit deeper, we can hear the entire Gospel in this text. Here is no hard and cruel "must," but a blessed "may." God has released us from the nothingness in which we formerly lived. He has redeemed us from the futility of life. He has given us a goal, in the achievement of which we can forget ourselves, a goal which gives an eternal glow to even the poorest of human lives. Let us stand quietly before this gift of God and meditate upon the two truths to which the Apostle testifies:

1. There is an indestructible crown for which we may strive.

2. This gives an immeasurable value to even the most pitiful human life.

I.

God has placed an indestructible goal before our lives, that enables us to forget all lesser ones. That is the first fact. Paul pictures it to us by reminding us of the greatest moment in the athletic life of the ancient world, the awarding of the prizes at the Olympic games of Greece. Paul was probably one of the thousands who had witnessed this dramatic scene. There upon an elevated place stood the victors. The best blood of Hellas, strong and handsome because of the hard discipline and thorough training to which their bodies had been subjected. For years they had prepared themselves for this moment. Now it had arrived. Acclaimed by the wild applause of the whole nation, the victors were crowned with a simple circlet of the sacred laurel. That unassuming chaplet was regarded as being of infinitely higher worth than had it been a circlet of solid gold. It was sufficient to engrace the wearer's name deeply in the memory of his people. Even in our own day, tablets are excavated on which the names of these victors are recorded. Every Grecian boy dreamed of the day when he might stand there with the triumphal wreath about his forehead, as he received the plaudits of all Greece. The whole nation was proud of its best sons. Its acclaim was similar to that which we gave to the young woman who swam the English Channel, who returned to her home to find that an admiring populace had covered it with flowers.

And here Paul says that God has placed a similar goal, although a far greater one, before our lives. *Now they do it to obtain a corruptible crown; but we an incorruptible.* It is an unending and undeserving gift that God has given us—the possibility of obtaining an incorruptible and undefiled inheritance. God might have given us over to destruction. He might have cast us aside as a potter discards a defective, an unusable vase. God could have created a new world out of new matter, without us. But He did not. He did not let us sink into the flood of our sin and hopelessness. He descended to us, in Christ, that we might be elevated from the futility of our existence. He wants us to take part in the new world which He will create and for which He is now preparing. We cannot yet see of what this new creation will consist; that we shall experience later. But when we read the Scriptures it is often as if rays of light can be seen through small openings in a door. God gives us repeated hints of what He has in mind. For example, in the Parable of the Talents, we read: *Well done, good and faithful servant; thou hast been faithful over a few things, I will make thee ruler over many things*: God, then, does not intend us for mere psalm singing and rest. *I will make thee ruler over many things!* God has entrusted us with some tasks here, but He will give us greater ones than any we have thus far received.

This is true even in the world of athletics. Only those who have achieved recognition in the preliminary contests of their own land are selected for international competition. Only these are admitted to the circle of those who strive for world leadership. It is true, also, in much higher sense, in the redemptive plan of God. Only those can become a part of the new world of God who have overcome *this* world. We can enter this kingdom with its greater tasks only when we have mastered this life. We can be entrusted with eternity only when we have passed through the battle of this age as conquerors, when we have received the crown of victory of which Paul speaks at the end of his life, *I have fought a good fight, I have finished my course, I have kept the faith: henceforth there is laid up for me a crown of righteousness.* It is this of which Jesus speaks in the *Book of Revelation. To him that overcometh will I grant to sit with Me in My throne, even as I also overcame and am now set down with My Father in His throne.* Undeserved grace! He, the Conqueror of the world, invites us to sit with Him as conquerors.

II.

If that be true; if such a possibility is open to us through the redemptive work of the Savior; if this star shines above us, our life possesses immeasurable value. Even the most miserable human existence is given an incorruptible glory and a serious responsibility.

If our life had no end but darkness, we should have

no need to take it seriously. We could do with it what we wished. We could conceive of it as a joke which someone had played on us. At its end, we could throw away the costume we have worn, as one throws a clown suit after a Hallowe'en ball. Life would then be no more than an interesting stroll through a harvest field, with the only matter of importance being how much one sees and takes along. But it is entirely different if the Apostle is right—if God has placed an incorruptible crown before us as the goal of life. Then we are compelled to say that everyone that enters this life begins a race, whether he is conscious of it or not. He enters an arena that all others—even the heroes of faith in Apostolic days—have entered, to begin a race in which he must be either a winner or a loser. *Know ye not that they which run in a race run all?* asks Paul.

And the most serious part of the matter is that each of us can run but once. The peoples of the Orient believe that we live many lives upon the earth. They think that it is possible to attempt the struggle anew, after having lost the first encounter. The poet Lessing also believed in the possibility of such rebirth. Oh, if it were really so, if we could once more begin from the beginning! How differently we would arrange our lives! How we should strive to utilize the experiences which had been ours in our first existence, in order to make the second better! But this is only a wishful phantasy. We run this race but *once*. We have but one chance to win. One struggle determines our eternal fate. Each

of us is young but once. Only once does each of us
engage in that momentous struggle with his own nature
which must determine whether he is to be the master or
servant of his natural impulses. Only once do we enter
maturity with its struggle for influence and position, in
which we must show whether we are men or broken
shadows. Only once do we pass each succeeding stage
of life's race. That is why every day is valuable. It
would seem as though the people of our day are pecul-
iarly conscious of this single chance and consequent
value of life. This is largely the explanation of the
hurry and bustle that occupies present-day business and
society. It is as though over the whole of our modern
life is written, *They . . . run all.* But they run only for
a corruptible wreath, while we strive for an incorruptible crown. But each of us may run only once. Each can
engage in the struggle with the world only once. The
world strains every nerve to conquer us. It seeks to
entice and then to frighten us, that it may make us its
captive. It is this struggle which decides whether we
shall come to the goal of life as victors or losers, like
moths the wings of which have been singed by the flames
of worldly desires.

What must we do in order to become victors? We
all know something of the military tactics used when an
attack is to be made upon an enemy front. All available
forces are massed at the point at which the assault is to
be made. Troops are withdrawn from other sectors,

where they are not absolutely needed, and used in a united attack upon the enemy's lines. It is to this simple law of strategy that Paul refers when he says, *Every man that striveth for the mastery is temperate in all things.* The Greek youths who participated in the athletic games were old enough to have enjoyed the pleasures of life. They had taken part in many festivals, banquets and dances with their friends. But now a greater goal filled their vision, the conquest for a corruptible wreath of glory. Everything which heretofore had filled their lives was pushed into the background. Not because they no longer found pleasure in these things. Their temperate life had but one reason—their youthful resources must be conserved for the *one* decisive struggle. All their competitive powers must be concentrated upon this one purpose and everything else subordinated. All their powers had to be directed toward this one goal.

In all this, we are precisely like the young men of ancient Greece. As soon as we are strongly impressed with our eternal destiny so that we recognize why we are here, our attitude toward all the harmless pleasures of life is suddenly changed. Not that we have no more pleasure in beautiful things which this world offers us to see and enjoy. Not that we find no joy in pleasant companionships and good music. He who can participate in these without harm to his spiritual life can do so. No Protestant Christian can dictate to another in these things. Each of us must make these decisions for himself. But I may place before you this question: Can we nonchalantly take part in these pleasures, when we have come properly to understand how valuable every day of this life is—when we see how infinitely much depends upon our victory or defeat in the struggle with the temptations of this world Can we unconcernedly dance a night away, while at the same time there are, in any nearby city, people who must spend their nights in the street because they can find no home and others are driven in desperation to take their own life? I do no more than ask the question if it is possible. Each of us must give an answer to his own conscience. Can we continue our careless enjoyment of these things, (when once we have come to see that this life is not a pleasure trip but a contest, in which we can conquer only if we are willing to sacrifice everything that we may obtain the pearl of great price? Does not the thought come to us: What would become of me if in the midst of these things I were called suddenly into the presence of God?

[On a certain fateful occasion a famous actress attended a costume ball. During a pause between dances she turned to her companion and, driven by a fleeting fancy, said, "I have often pretended to die on the stage, but, as you see, I am still alive." A few minutes later she collapsed; shortly afterwards she was dead!] Do we think that we shall come to the goal as victors if we pass from "this life" under such conditions? Paul was scourged five times, stoned once, thrice beaten with rods. He lived in *weariness and painfulness, in watchings often, in hunger and thirst, in fastings often, in cold and nakedness;* but near the end of his life he still said, *Not as though I had already attained, either were already perfect: but I press on, if that I may lay hold on that for which also I was lain hold on by Christ Jesus.* If Paul, after a lifetime of sacrifice, was still uncertain if he would reach the goal, can we believe that we, after we have gleefully danced our way through life, will be awarded the victor's laurels? If that seems doubtful to us, then it should be clear that many things in our life which in themselves are quite innocent, take away something of the strength which we should use to become victors in life. The goal can be reached only through the consecration of our whole life. Even the good pearls must be sacrificed in order to secure the pearl of good price. *I count all things but loss for the excellency of the knowledge of Christ Jesus my Lord: for Whom I have suffered the loss of all things, and do count them but dung that I may win Christ and be found in Him.* Eternal life can never be won unless we are willing to devote this earthly life to its attainment.

It is only from this point that we can understand the most difficult occurrences in our lives. It seems incomprehensible that it is the noblest people who must pass through the greatest suffering. It would be unintelligible if the meaning of this life were to be found in itself. A solution comes to us only as we remember that this life is a contest that will determine who will reach the victor's goal where God can use him for still greater tasks. Even in the realm of sport there is a special race—a handicap race—in which the course leads through the marshes, across ditches and through thickets. All these obstacles are carefully planned. The winner in such a race must have learned to conquer such difficulties. So also God places intentional barriers in our life's course—someone with whom we must work and whose personality is a continued irritant; an occupation that we detest or a bodily limitation such as *the thorn in the flesh,* from which repeated prayers did not release Paul. Virtually every human life has such obstacles to overcome, restrictions that will cause our unselfishness to die. Death, itself, may become very difficult for even a mature Christian, so that he may plead, "Pray that God may release me, for I can no longer bear this suffering."

We have been permitted to consider with quiet thankfulness the glorious gift of God in giving us a goal to which we can give ourselves utterly. We have also sensed the responsibility that this lays upon our life. In the Grecian games the racers were surrounded by a great throng of spectators in the arena, who encouraged the competitors with their cries. The contest in which we are engaged has also its observers. Jesus said, *There is joy in the presence of the angels of God over one sinner that repenteth.* The heavenly world and the multitude of Christian victors are watching our struggle and, like a great cloud of witnesses, encourage us to greater endeavor. Because of this, let us place our lives anew beneath the word, *Be thou faithful unto death, and I will give thee a crown of life.*

IX.

THE MIRROR OF GOD'S WORD

Wherefore lay apart all filthiness and superfluity of naughtiness, and receive with meekness the engrafted Word, which is able to save your souls. But be ye doers of the Word, and not hearers only, deceiving your own selves. For if any be a hearer of the Word and not a doer, he is like unto a man beholding his face in a glass: For he beholdeth himself, and goeth his way, and straightway forgetteth what manner of man he was. But whoso looketh into the perfect law of liberty, and continueth therein, he being not a forgetful hearer, but a doer of the work, this man shall be blessed in his deed. If any man among you seem to be religious, and bridleth not his tongue, but deceiveth his own heart, this man's religion is vain. Pure religion and undefiled before God and the Father, is this, To visit the fatherless and widows in their affliction, and to keep himself unspotted from the world.

JAMES 1: 21-27

IX.

THE MIRROR OF GOD'S WORD

OF THE many temples and mosques, in which people worship, it is a very simple one which made the deepest impression upon me. It is one I saw in Japan. An amazingly large room, almost entirely empty, no statues of deities, no pictures, no decorations, no altar. There was only one object in the entire temple, a round mirror hanging on one wall. The people who knelt in prayer and who cowered in the dark corners of the room, lowered their eyes in fearful reverence before the object. "What is the significance of this mirror?" I asked. I was told that it represented the eye of a divinity, the token of his presence. I could not help but think of that word of James which also speaks of a mirror, from which we humans would gladly flee. The mirror is the Word of God. This amazing world which surrounds us seems, indeed, to be an enormous, dark room. Nowhere is there an image of God that we can touch; nowhere anything that proves to us that God exists. We cannot see God nor make any image of Him. But in the great room of this world there is also a place where a mirror hangs. When we look into it we are enveloped by the presence of God and we see ourselves both as we really are and as we should be. But when we do what we see there, we find God and are blessed

in our deed. Let us pause before the wonderful gift
which God has given us in His Word, in the Word which
became flesh in His Son and which speaks to us whenever we open the Bible. Let us lay to heart what the
Apostle says about this mirror of the Word. We may
sum up his thought in two sentences:

1. We must gaze into this mirror much more earnestly than heretofore;

2. We must translate into action that which we see,
in order that we may be blessed in our deed.

I.

We are to gaze into this mirror. Perhaps it has
been difficult for us to understand why people, who are
spiritually much more advanced than we, should have
taken time to spend hours each day in the reading of
this old Book. Luther spent three or four hours each
day in prayerful study of the Bible. When Michael-
angelo was painting his immortal pictures on the ceiling
of the Sistine Chapel he read Dante's *Divine Comedy*
and the Bible: and when one sees these pictures, it is
clear that they were painted by a man who, for months,
read nothing else. Why is it that people, who stand so
far above us spiritually and artistically, could not read
enough in this old volume, that they devoted costly
morning hours to a study of these ancient histories and
homilies. There are many books more fascinating,
books which stimulate our imagination to a greater ex-
tent. It is a great mistake to seek in the Bible a gripping

transcript of human life. We have any number of fascinating books which carry us along with irresistible power and that absorb us to the point of self-forgetfulness. The Bible is not intended to be a fascinating book. The intention of it is the very opposite. It is not planned to so absorb us that we shall forget ourselves. It is planned to do just the opposite. The Bible is a mirror in which we see ourselves as we really are. A mirror is not a photograph which can be retouched and unpleasant characteristics removed. A portrait painter also can flatter a sitter by leaving out of his composition unpleasant realities. But a mirror is painfully honest. Pitilessly it shows us our own face. God has given us a mirror in which we can see our true condition. The eyes of eternity are directed at us. We see ourselves as God sees us, as we shall see ourselves, finally, in the hour of death.

The opening chapters of the Bible show us the first human beings as they hide among the trees of the garden from the presence of God; and the last book of the Bible, *Revelation,* shows us the last people as they hide themselves in the dens of the mountains and say to the rocks, *Fall on us and hide us from the face of Him that sitteth on the throne and from the wrath of the Lamb.* From the beginning of this volume to the end we see man as he really is. And each of us who dwells long with the Bible and who penetrates deeply into this wonderful Book will reproduce the experience of David, when Nathan came to him and told him the story of the

rich man who had stolen the only lamb of his neighbor.
To his horror David saw his true self in the mirror of
this story. He became conscious of the abyss of evil
into which he had fallen. Every man who associates
with the Bible will feel as did the non-Christian who on
having heard the story of the Prodigal Son said, "The
man who wrote that must have known *me*, for it is an
exact description of my life. The poor fellow who
could not lose his yearning for home is myself. The
story is my history." As we become better acquainted
with the Bible there are two things which happen simul-
taneously: God becomes increasingly great and we become correspondingly small. With every day He becomes more wonderful and more incomprehensible. We
cannot understand that God, in His Son, should have
concerned Himself with us. We realize more and more
our unworthiness of this grace. It becomes increasingly
difficult for us to understand that God has had mercy
upon people like ourselves.

If this is the purpose of the Bible—to be a mirror
in which we see ourselves as God always sees us and
as we may see ourselves before death—then we can understand why attacks have been made against it, as
against no other book in the world. It is a criticism such
as has been directed against no other volume of world
literature. I do not refer to the serious historical in-
vestigations that have concerned themselves with the
Biblical books, but with the attacks made upon the inner
content of the Bible. Why this bitter struggle against

the Bible? Humanity has rebelled against this Book. We should like to scatter the mirror that shows us our true face. But that is an impossibility. We cannot push the Bible to one side; we cannot break the mirror. We read in our text, *In a humble spirit receive that Word which has been planted in you.* (Luther's Translation.) We cannot eradicate this Word which has been planted in us. It does not merely come to us from the outside. It has become a part of us from within. Nevertheless, people still make an attempt at ridiculing the Bible and, sometimes, use very ingenious schemes to bring it about.

Many of us are justifiably offended when we see some anti-religious magazine or book, pouring ridicule upon the Bible. But there is something worse than this ridicule—something of which many of us who are churchgoers stand guilty. It is that to which James refers when he speaks of people who are *Like unto a man beholding his natural face in a mirror: for he beholdeth himself and goeth his way, and straightway forgetteth what manner of man he was.* Such a man permits the mirror to remain. He makes no effort to destroy it. Time and again he passes it, but he has accustomed himself to glance so briefly and carelessly into it that the image makes no impression upon him, and he forgets, almost instantly, what he has seen. Is not the gravest fault in our modern spiritual life, seriously reflected in our attitude toward the Bible? Why do so many of us remain hungry and unsatisfied in the midst

of what appear to be stirring impressions? Is it not
because these so-called impressions do not really impress; because our spirits are like slates upon which
words or pictures are drawn only to be almost immediately wiped away by the sponge of forgetfulness. We are
like a man who goes his way and straightway forgets
what he has seen. That is why we remain spiritually im-
poverished in the midst of a wealth of stimuli. This
manifests itself particularly in our relationship to the
Word of God. It is tragic to recall what a wealth of
words have passed over us in the years that we have attended church—God's Words, words of life, eternal
words, words that possess enough power to change our
lives completely! We have established the habit of
hearing these words and straightway forgetting them; of
looking into the mirror during a fleeting moment of reverence and then going our way forgetting how we had
appeared therein.

In the Parable of the Sower Jesus speaks of the
birds that pick up the seeds that fall on the beaten path-
way. A hungry flock comes and carries everything away.
These birds are the new impressions that storm upon us
when we leave the church, when we meet our friends
and converse with them. *Then cometh the wicked one
and catcheth away that which was sown in his heart.*
Behind the flightiness and superficiality of our rapidly-
moving generation, stands the dark Power which seeks
to rob us of our salvation. That Power sends a flock of
fluttering birds to carry away the seed before it can be-

come grounded and rooted in our hearts. This superficial reception and forgetting of the truths of Scripture
is worse than open enmity against the Bible. What can
we do to conquer this forgetfulness that prevents the
seeds of eternity from penetrating the soil of the heart?

The Apostle says, *Whoso looketh into* (or, as it is
literally, *who bows himself under) the perfect law of
liberty and continueth therein, he being not a forgetful
hearer but a doer of the work, this man shall be blessed
in his deed.* We dare not suppose that a hasty glance is
enough to secure the divine power in the Word. Even
in the secular world there is nothing great or worth-
while that a man can accomplish at one leap or that he
can penetrate with a fleeting glance. Even if musically
gifted, one is compelled to listen carefully and repeatedly, before he can grasp the theme and composition of
a great symphony and understand the relationship of its
various parts. Richard Wagner had to study the basic
principles of harmony seven different times before he
mastered them. Surely we cannot suppose that the
greatest thing that we have, the Book of books, the treasury of divine mysteries, will unfold its treasures to a
hurried or casual observer! To be sure, it sometimes
happens that a man hears a word of the Bible and finds
salvation, then and there. During the cholera plague in
London a pastor was called into a haunt of criminals.
There a man, who was lying at death's door, said to
him, "During my criminal activity as a burglar, I once

happened to enter your church and there I heard a word which I have never forgotten and which I should like to hear once more." It was a verse from Psalm 139: *Whither shall I go from Thy spirit? Or whither shall I flee from Thy presence?* In the mirror of this psalm the man had seen his whole life as it really was, a great offense to the Spirit of God. And there, at the last moment, he found peace. But that is a very unusual manifestation of grace. In most instances we must familiarize ourselves with the Word for a long time and with many prayers before we can really look into it. One of the most noteworthy words in the Bible and one deserving of our lifelong attention, is this, *Whoso looketh into the perfect law of liberty and continueth therein . . . shall be blessed in his deed.*

At first, our minds do not penetrate this Book. When we begin to read the Bible it seems as though we step into a dark passage, closed in on both sides by black walls. We hear such stern words as: *Enter ye in the strait gate,* and *If any man will come after Me, Let him deny himself,* and, *Whosoever shall smite thee on thy right cheek, turn to him the other also.* On all sides of us are black walls, difficult commandments that would hem us in. Many people are frightened away by these hard sayings. But, says the Apostle, *Whoso . . . continueth therein,* who ceases not from going obediently in the same direction, will have the great experience of seeing a point of light at the end of the dark passage, a light that grows larger and brighter as he continues.

And then he discovers this light is the light of day. It marks the entrance into the open air. If we but cast a hurried glance, everything seems to be dark, but if we continue to look, our eyes penetrate to the light. We see *into the perfect law of liberty*. That is, we see that behind all these commandments and behind all these difficult tasks which God gives us, there stands a purpose, and that purpose is our liberty. God wants to free us from ourselves. He wants to make us free from the fetters which bind us to earth. He wants to remove the things which enchain our spirits to unworthy goals and hereby set us free to attain the great goal He has prepared for us. An enchained heart cannot soar heavenward. The most painful experiences of our life, those in which we lose something to which our heart clings, are ways to liberty. Servitum Dei est summa libertas. "To serve God is the highest freedom." So we must look into, bow ourselves beneath, and penetrate through *the perfect law of liberty*.

II.

But when we gaze earnestly and long into the mirror, we cannot be satisfied with mere looking, not even with meditation and an emotional response. Our looking must necessarily result in acting. It is only in the deed that we shall be blessed. That is the second thing which James has to tell us.

So long as we but glance superficially into this mirror, we shall attain nothing more than an attitude of reverance or a pious emotion.   There are people who shed tears whenever they hear the story of the Passion of our Lord. We have today a movement in our church which is seeking to create liturgical services that shall be emotionally fruitful and artistically complete. Who is there that would not applaud this purpose! And yet, when we see into the mirror of the Word, into this frank mirror that reveals our true nature, we are frightened by that which the Bible repeatedly says of a worship that does not result in action. Isaiah observed a great festival of the Old Testament, which was much more impressive and awe-inspiring than our modern services of worship.   The smoke of the sacrifices ascended to the honor of God. Clouds of incense rose to heaven. White robed priests went here and there in accordance with an ancient ritual, while the entire populace knelt in reverent silence.   But Isaiah says, *Hear the Word of the Lord . . . . To what purpose is the multitude of your sacrifices unto Me? saith the Lord: I am full of the burnt offerings of rams and the fat of fed beasts; and I delight not in the blood of bullocks or of lambs or of he goats . . . . incense is an abomination unto Me; the new moons and sabbaths, the calling of assemblies, I cannot away with . . . . And when ye spread forth your hands, I will hide mine eyes from you: yea, when ye make many prayers, I will not hear; your hands are full of blood.*

Why such strong words directed against a religious celebration?   God cannot bear and will not hearken to

our worship and our prayers if the life which we lead
at home or in our place of business stands in contrast to
that which we profess in the church. They are an abomination unto Him. God can receive a miserable sinner
if he is honest, but a liar he cannot receive. That is so
among human beings, also. We are not unwilling to
give something to a beggar, even when he seems to be
quite worthless. But if he lies to us, and we are aware
of his lying, our sympathy instantly turns cold. But in
God's eyes we appear as liars if we fold our hands and
pray and then proceed to act in a way directly alien to
prayer. Let us look more deeply into the mirror which
God holds before our eyes and by it test our lives! *If
any man among you thinketh himself to be religious,
and bridleth not his own tongue, but deceiveth his own
heart, this man's religion is vain.* If after church we go
home and create a scene at the dinner table, let fall
some barbed word which, like a sharp arrow, wounds
another, then our worship is vain. It would have been
better had we stayed at home. We should, at least, have
been saved an act of dishonesty. If in church we sing
and pray, and, later, permit our tongue to indulge itself
in slander concerning someone we do not like and whom
we seek to injure, then our worship is a lie, we deceive
our own heart, and our religion is vain. That man is a
liar who is one sort of man in church, where with pious
look he sits in the company of fellow worshipers, and
another sort in the factory, where he inflicts his bad
temper upon his subordinates; or who, in the family
circle, plays the part of a petty tyrant and makes life

miserable for his wife. Such a man is an abomination
unto God. Have not some of us noticed that when we
sought God in prayer—in a moment of emergency it
may have been at the sick bed of a loved one—that
the heavens seemed closed? We have beaten upon the
door and it was not opened. God hid His face from us.
Then was His word fulfilled for us: *When ye spread
forth your hands, I will hide My eyes from you . . . .
Your hands are full of blood.* Perhaps we have wounded
someone who waited for a friendly word. As long as
any bitterness toward a brother remains in our heart
God cannot hear us. No matter how desperately we may
cry to Him, His ear is deaf to our cry.

But just as definitely as God closes the door when
we come to Him as hypocrites, so heartily does He receive us and open to us all His treasures, as soon as He
sees that we are earnestly ready to do, at least, the sim-
plest things He commands in His word. Our pious meditation, in itself, makes no impression upon God, for it
touches only the soul's surface. God hears but one
language, the language of deeds. The word which does
not issue in deeds has no value. *Pure religion and undefiled before God and the Father is this, To visit the
fatherless and widows in their affliction, and to keep
himself unspotted from the world.* Such a religion will
make us blessed in our deeds.

There is, then, a blessed worship in which everyone
of us can participate, even the least fortunate, who are
excluded from all earthly joys. This pure religion is not
observed in a cathedral, amid the ringing of bells and

the singing of choirs, nor in a concert hall where we are carried away by glorious music. It is a religion for tenement rooms, where an eccentric old woman needs someone to read to her. As we serve her, we practice this pure and undefiled religion. And it is a religion for an institution for the feeble-minded. If we live with, and serve these poor people who have lost friends and family, we perform the blessed worship of which the Apostle speaks. Or when we help lonesome people —when we do not hesitate to climb steep, dark staircases to seek someone whom others avoid, that, too, is pure and undefiled religion. Nobody, possibly, knows or cares anything about it; the newspapers will not report it. From a human standpoint, such helpful services to the unfortunate make little difference to those about us. Everyone who has gone his way knows that by treading it he assumes a burden that will often not permit him to sleep of nights. Nevertheless, James tells us, *This man shall be blessed in his deed.* Wherever unselfish and hidden help is given, there the gates of heaven are opened. The things which separate people one from another in this life, begin to disappear. We begin to realize that an inescapable relationship still exists between us all. We have a foretaste of the new world of God. For blessedness does not consist in external possessions. These are but temporal and temporary satisfactions. Blessedness consists in this—that our weak human will is lost in God's will, like a little stream in the great ocean. The man in whom all opposition to God has vanished, is already blessed.

We have spoken of the mirror which God has given us in God's holy Word. Let us look deeply into it, until we see clearly the perfect law of liberty. And when we have seen it, let us translate into action the vision vouchsafed us. Then shall we, beyond all peradventure be blessed in our deed!

X.

VICTORIOUS PRAYER

Then when Mary was come where Jesus was, and saw Him, she fell down at His feet, saying unto Him, Lord, if thou hadst been here, my brother had not died. When Jesus therefore saw her weeping, and the Jews also weeping which came with her, He groaned in the spirit and was troubled, and said, Where have ye laid him? They said unto Him, Lord, come and see. Jesus wept. Then said the Jews, Behold how He loved him! And some of them said, Could not this man, which opened the eyes of the blind, have caused that even this man should not have died? Jesus therefore, again groaning in Himself cometh to the grave. It was a cave, and a stone lay upon it. Jesus said, Take ye away the stone. Martha, the sister of him that was dead, saith unto Him, Lord, by this time he stinketh: for he hath been dead four days. Jesus saith unto her, Said I not unto thee that, if thou wouldest believe, thou shouldest see the glory of God? Then they took away the stone from the place where the dead was laid. And Jesus lifted up His eyes and said, Father, I thank Thee that Thou hast heard Me. And I knew that Thou hearest Me always: But because of the people which stand by I said it, that they may believe that Thou hast sent Me. And when He thus had spoken, He cried with a loud voice, Lazarus, come forth. And he that was dead came forth, bound hand and foot with grave-clothes: and his face was bound about with a napkin. Jesus saith unto them, Loose him, and let him go.

JOHN 11: 32-45

X.

VICTORIOUS PRAYER

SOME FORTY years ago Ernest Haeckel prophesied that, although the churches would not be destroyed by the advance of natural science, they would yet be cleared of all old furnishings. Their place would be taken, he said, by a great aquarium in the chancel and interesting exhibits of animal life elsewhere in the edifice, to teach us that we should respect the unbreakable laws of nature.

Why has this rebuilding not yet taken place? Why are there still many thoughtful individuals who go to church? Does it represent only a flight from reality into a "better beyond"? No; it is the very growth of the natural sciences and the increasing insight into the laws upon which our lives depend, that have raised the question of life in a more demanding form, and have driven to the church many laboring and struggling people who must confront life. Simply, the question is whether or not we are entirely at the mercy of these natural laws. If a physician should locate an internal cancer, that is beyond the aid which an operation might render, are we then merely hopeless victims of the process of disease which leads slowly to a painful death? Is this life really a pitiless struggle for existence, in which the stronger rules and the weaker is mercilessly trodden

underfoot?   Are we helpless in the presence of these
facts, or is there some way of escape?   Is there a power
to which we can turn that is stronger than these necessities of natural law?   More strongly than ever, we are
convinced that "only" if there is such a power, which
is stronger than the whole world, can we continue this
struggle of life.   Otherwise we have no other choice
than to adjust ourselves unwillingly to the inevitable.

The question whether there is such a world-conquer-
ing power is more pressing for us, than for any preced-
ing generation.   It is this question which drives people
to church.   Here they seek to establish contact with an
invisible world.   Even if it be but for an hour, they
want to touch these invisible streams of power which are
stronger than the necessities of this difficult life and
which make it possible for us to master the exacting demands of daily life.   Our text meets precisely this need
of modern man.   For with it we are comforted, not
merely by the thought of the future life, glorious as this
comfort may be.   Rather does Jesus, in this scene, stand
as God's champion in the midst of the deadly powers of
earthly reality.   He pits Himself against a condition
which seems to us to be unchangeable.   He halts, by His
might, a process that, otherwise, would have continued
irresistibly.   His hand reaches directly into the hard
realities of this present world.   In the light of our text,
let us consider Jesus' power of prayer, as revealed at
the grave of Lazarus:

1. Its basis.

2. How we, as His church, can participate in it.

I.

Even in our small human relationships there is something great about a man who, despite the fact of his being opposed, rejected and ridiculed on every side, moves toward his goal without swerving and with high assurance. That is how Columbus followed his ideal, even though the leaders of his own day thought him a fool. Zeppelin made the same gesture when everyone in Wuerttenburg laughed at the "crazy Count." He continued with his experiences until he reached the goal which he had set for himself. But greater far than any such as these is the solitary yet triumphal action of Jesus, that is pictured in our text. Every power was massed against Him to hold Him back and to convince Him of the impossibility of His plans. He stepped into the midst of a hopeless company of mourners, *Jesus therefore saw her weeping and the Jews also weeping which came with her.* We know only too well, something of this heartbreaking weeping at the grave. When, for example, we see orphaned children stand beside the grave of their mother. Their weeping makes us thoroughly conscious of our absolute impotence in the presence of death. Even Mary, who of all those present stood nearest to Jesus and who believed in His saving power, could in this moment address Him only in the desolate words of complaint, *Lord, if Thou hadst been here, my brother had not died.* Which was as much as to say, "You are too late. You can do nothing to help your friend now. If You had come a week earlier, You might have saved him, but that time is past." But the attack upon Jesus does not come solely from those about Him, who in despairing submission bow before the powerful king of terrors. For the most startling fact in this story is that Jesus Himself does not stand as an immovable and untouched rock. He is stirred to the heart. *He groaned in the spirit and was troubled, and said, Where have ye laid him? They said unto Him, Lord, come and see. Jesus wept.*

Goethe could never be brought to look upon the corpse of a friend. He wanted to avoid this disturbing fact as far as possible. He knew how the memory of the dead follows us through many nights and days. Christ became our brother in this, also, that He did not avoid this terrifying experience. He overcame its sorrow. But while He wept, the Jews, these bitter critics of His every act, took advantage of the situation. Even in this moment they sought to discourage Him by their remarks. *Could not this man, which opened the eyes of the blind, have caused that even this man should not have died?* They subscribed to the charge that in this decisive hour He had come too late. And even in the last moment, when Jesus had overcome all these negative influences, and when He was about to command that the grave be opened, Martha, the dead man's sister, tries to restrain Him: *Lord, by this time he stinketh: for he hath been dead four days.* Leave the grave alone! You are trying to do the impossible. Decomposition has already begun! Many of us know from our experience in the War the devastating effect upon a company of soldiers when a turn of the wind carried to them the horrible odor of the unburied dead on the battlefield. This breath of death, perhaps more than anything else, forces us to realize the nearness and the horrible power of death.

But while the grave stands open and the odor of death smites Him, and while He is surrounded by the tearstained faces and reddened eyes of the mourners, *Jesus lifted up His eyes and said, Father, I thank Thee that Thou hast heard Me.* Furtwaengler, a Christian artist of our own day, has attempted to picture this moment, when (as so often in the miracles recorded by John) Jesus lifted up His eyes to the Father. The picture is very simple. The eye of God is overhead, in the midst of a boundless star-sprinkled heaven. Before Him on the dark earth, stands the Son. And now the flashing eye of the Son meets the eye of the Father. The Son's gaze penetrates through everything until it rests on the Creator. And in the moment in which the Father and the Son gaze into each other's eyes, the opposition of the world becomes insignificant. The whole of nature, with its changeable laws, lies in the hand of God, even as on the morn of creation. It is as soft clay in the hands of the potter. He can shape it as He will. There can be no opposition. There is here no struggle against an invincible opponent. There remains only a thanksgiving for the victory that has been won. *Jesus lifted up His eyes and said, Father, I thank Thee that Thou hast heard Me.* When the eye of the only begotten Son found the eye of the Father, the battle was won. Everything which happened thereafter was only the fruit of the victory. It follows the thanksgiving of Jesus as thunder follows lightning. *And when He thus had spoken, He cried with a loud voice, Lazarus, come forth. And he that was dead came forth.*

II.

When we observe this triumphant act of Jesus, every step which is the result of prayer; when we see how unwaveringly He strides through all the obstacles which are placed before Him, we cannot but realize the distance that we are from Him. We realize how far short we come of really victorious prayer. Every day we must deal with the same Power that Jesus opposed. It is a Power that seeks to destroy us, body and soul. In every possible form it seeks to discourage us and break our power of resistance. It may be physical suffering which thwarts and hinders us. It may be an unsatisfactory family relationship which shatters our life. It may be some mental hazard or some business care, which, at the moment, seems to rise before us like an impassable mountain. Behind all these things lurks the enemy who seeks our destruction. *The last enemy is death.* We should have a victorious certainty as we meet him, so that we can pass over into the dark without wavering. We should go prayerfully into that which lies before us. We should have the assurance with which Jesus brushed past all obstacles, until He stood at the grave of Lazarus. But how weak and uncertain we are! We are torn by doubts. We are discouraged by the critical and hopeless comments of our fellow men. And we know the reason for our wavering attitude. We lack the flashing eye with which Jesus gazed into the eye of the Father. There is something between God and us. We are fallen creatures. We become particularly conscious of this when we see someone die. How far we are removed from God, how deep we have fallen, that God must lay upon us such a fearful struggle! We become aware of the strength of death. We feel that everything is at stake. We know, then, that we are separated from the Source of life and stand under God's judgment.

Our text is a splendid illustration of the way in which Jesus supports His doubting and wavering disciples by the powers of His prayers. Martha is a vivid example of the wavering attitude which usually possesses us. She knew Jesus very well. He was a frequent visitor at her home. But when He said to her, *Thy brother shall rise again,* her answer was, *I know that he shall rise again in the resurrection at the last day.* Yes, *at the last day,* at the end of all earthly time, her faith could visualize a possible pictory over death. But that this victory was possible now, in that very moment, was something she could not grasp. That is how most of us feel. We can believe that Christ is sent by God, perhaps, and that at the end of time there is an existence in which death is conquered. But that Christ is able to interrupt the processes of nature, so as to snatch its booty from death's hands at the last moment, that is too much for us to believe. That is impossible. We cannot possibly accept that. That which stood in the way of Martha's faith is precisely the same thing which limits and destroys our prayer every day, the conviction of the immutibility of natural law. *Lord, by this time he stinketh: for he hath been dead four days!* The process of dissolution goes its resistless way. Nothing more can be done. We must resign ourselves to the inevitable.

So we see a person who has become the slave of drink, sinking steadily step by step as the process of alcoholic poisoning continues. We simply cannot believe that he can be saved. Or, if we ourselves have suffered one defeat after another in connection with a specific sin, each defeat leaves us weaker than before. We know that we are steadily losing our power of resistance to certain temptations and we feel ourselves upon the steep descent which leads to ultimate tragedy. We may perhaps hold to the belief that beyond death there is another existence, but we cannot believe that even in this life everything can once more become new. That is the decisive point over which our faith does not pass.

What does Jesus say to those who cannot overcome the doubt that is born from this overwhelming impression of the inevitability of natural law? Jesus does not reject us. He knows our weakness. To His questioning disciple He speaks a wonderful word, which is at the same time spoken to us all, *Said I not unto Thee, that, if thou wouldest believe, thou shouldest see the glory of God?* This reminds us of His words to the father of the boy who was possessed of a dumb spirit, under whose influence he was dashed to the ground and foamed at the mouth. The father had lost hope of any possible recovery, but the Lord said, *If thou canst believe, all things are possible to him that believeth.* His words to Martha are, *Said I not unto thee?* If we were to believe without seeing because of some human word, faith would be a gamble, a leap into the dark, an adventure beyond our strength. But upon *His* word we can take the step, for behind it stands the full power of His atoning work. When He demands our faith, He supports us by the power of His prayers.

If thou wouldest believe, thou shouldest see the glory of God. So we must believe, before we may see. But we would like to reverse the order. First, we want to see, to be thoroughly convinced, to determine all possibilities; then make our careful calculations. First, we must see if the ice will support us without danger. Only then will we put our weight upon it. But God cannot make matters so easy for us. For then we should always remain in ourselves and the prisoners of earth. We could never reach the highest for which we have been created. We should never soar to the heights for which God has given us wings. We should never attain the blessedness of which God speaks in His last Beatitude, *Blessed are they that have not seen, and yet have believed.* If we would find God, the invisible God, Who surrounds us as does the air and Whom we yet cannot see, something must take place that is contrary to our natural wishes. Luther has said, "Prayer is like a small boat that climbs a mountain." God hides His face behind the clouds. He conceals Himself behind the seemingly unchanging processes of nature, behind the pitiless course of an illness, behind the power of death. He does this that we may learn to press through all hindrances to Him. That is why the Kingdom of God rests upon the ordinance, which Jesus impressed upon Martha, that we can see the glory of God *only* after we have first believed. This is the reason why so few find God. This rule is too daring for most people. Columbus, on his first voyage, had to endure days and weeks when he could not see any sign of land, when his vision was limited to a gray sea and an empty sky. Yet he could

not turn back. Only because he survived these difficult
weeks, supported only by the faith in his own heart,
could he experience the great moment when land rose
once more above the horizon. So in our lives, too, there
must be periods in which we cannot see, but only believe. Only afterward can we see the glorious deeds of
God, rising as great cliffs out of the sea.

We can experience the triumphant power of Christ
over all obstacles when we have learned, not to see, but
to pray and to believe, and to wait upon the Lord from
one morning watch until the other. Such waiting and
praying is not a leap into the dark, a chance in a lot-
tery, a reckless adventure. Neither is it a desperate
struggle for victory. It is the attitude with which Jesus,
at the grave of Lazarus, looked up at the Father. There
was no movement in the dark cave, from which the stone
had been rolled away. Nothing could be seen of the
power of God. Yet Jesus looked up to the Father and
said, *Father, I thank Thee that Thou hast heard Me,
And I know that Thou hearest Me always.* In like fashion we must begin all our prayers, *"Father, I thank
Thee,* that I am Thine and that Thou hast reconciled me
to Thee." Then we stand upon the ground of faith and
look up with faith's eye, as the Lord lifted His eyes to
the Father at Lazarus' grave.

Our text has shown us that we have a great Lord and
that we, as His church, shall be a part of a multitude of
victors, who are not afraid of the deathly powers which
threaten us on every side. We, too, may listen to the
word of a man of God in the Eighteenth Century, "Expect great things of God; attempt great things for God."

XI.

THE UNAVOIDABLE GOD

For I am not ashamed of the Gospel of Christ: for it is the power of God unto salvation to every one that believeth; to the Jew first, and also to the Greek. For therein is the righteousness of God revealed from faith to faith: as it is written, The just shall live by faith. For the wrath of God is revealed from heaven against all ungodliness and unrighteousness of men, who hold the truth in unrighteousness; because that which may be known of God is manifest in them; for God hath showed it unto them. For the invisible things of Him from the creation of the world are clearly seen, being understood through the things that are made, even His eternal power and Godhead; so that they are without excuse. Because that, when they knew God, they glorified Him not as God, neither were thankful; but became vain in their imaginations and their foolish heart was darkened. Professing themselves to be wise, they became fools, and changed the glory of the uncorruptible God into an image made like to corruptible man and to birds and fourfooted beasts and creeping things. Wherefore God also gave them up to uncleanness through the lusts of their own hearts, to dishonour their own bodies between themselves: who changed the truth of God into a lie, and worshipped and served the creature rather than the Creator, Who is blessed for ever. Amen.

ROMANS 1: 16-25

XI.

THE UNAVOIDABLE GOD

PAUL PLANS a journey to Rome, the seat of authority and culture. We sense from the words of our text that even before he set foot upon Italian soil, Paul felt, as one feels a distant earthquake, the powerful opposition which his message would meet, an opposition that was soon to find expression in the bloody persecutions of Nero. With this in mind, he writes, *I am not ashamed of the Gospel of Christ.* He faced the same opposition that we today experience, when, in our small way, we step out of the circle of our fellow believers and venture to say a word concerning God or Christ to someone who possesses greater educational or cultural advantages than ourselves. It is the same opposition which we, as a congregation and as a church experience if we are not content to remain in the company of believers, but present our testimony for Christ before a world in which a large majority rejects the Christian faith.

Never has opposition to the truth of the Gospel reached higher than in our day. It is a flood which reaches new levels with every passing hour. The persecutions of Christians by Nero, bloody as they were, and the attempt of Julian, the Apostate, once more to restore heathen worship in the Roman Empire, are almost insignificant, when compared with the persecution of

Christians in modern Russia. In five years, according to the plan of the Soviet government, every Christian church, sermon and school will have been eradicated in this, the largest of European lands, and all religious buildings converted into "exhibits for the godless," moving picture palaces and Bolshevist museums. If this plan prove successful, it would be impossible to isolate the waves. Is it not time, that in the presence of this universal and radical rejection of the Gospel of Christ, we Christians should withdraw from the public eye and devote our energies to the mutual edification of those who believe as we do? Ought we not to discontinue the attempt to force the Gospel upon a world which does not want it and which is aroused thereby to ever-increasing opposition? To this question Paul answers, that we cannot and dare not cease our efforts. Why may we not be discouraged by the world's opposition? Why may this oppositon not give us the right to leave the world to its fate and withdraw into the circle of fellow believers Why is it our duty to turn to all mankind with this Gospel, even in this day? Paul's answer to these questions is that all peoples, even when they completely reject God, are still in His power and must deal with Him whether they will or no. For we cannot escape God. There are, for us, but two possibilities:

1. Either God is against us, and gives us over to the lusts of our hearts;

2. Or God is for us, and we may then experience His saving power.

I.

Even in our opposition, in our rejection of God's invitation, we are forced to deal with Him. We sometimes think that in a period of unbelief God withdraws from the world which has turned its back upon Him. Perhaps we think that in a day when many are leaving the church, and in which there are large sections of our great cities in which no one goes to church, that God should have withdrawn behind the walls of the church, so that the millions who live without Him should lose His presence entirely. But Paul says, that such a thought is a mistake. He tells us something dreadful, which throws a searchlight upon many modern conditions. God works just as powerfully outside as inside the circle of believers. God is active in everything which occurs in our great cities—in the night clubs, in which young people waste their best powers and often become slaves of habits which wreck their whole future; in the lowest dens of crime and even in the "palaces of the godless," to which illuminated signs invite us. Behind them all, stands God. For what is it that takes place in such places? These people have rejected God, *wherefore God also gave them up to uncleanness, to the lusts of their own hearts, to dishonor their own bodies between themselves*

Like a flash of lightning this word reveals the dark side of modern city life. We sometimes ask ourselves the question, why it is that people, who have lost their inner strength, do not simply fall to the level of the brute. Why is it that they sink far below the animal and become the captives of a self-intoxication that ends

in the ruin of body and soul? Why is it that these moderns, who possess all the advantages of our technical
progress, make of their lives, not a harmonious existence, but a veritable hell, in which wild orgies are
followed by a despair which leads to the tragedy of
suicide? These things have a deep reason. They come
from God. God has created us for eternity. He has given
characteristics to our souls which render it possible for
us to give Him control over our lives and that enable
us to disregard anything that stands between us and our
eternal destiny. And He has also pointed out the way in
which we might find him. *Because that which may be
known of God is manifest . . . through the things that
were made.* Even when a person has been brought up
without any religious training, as is the case with millions of young people in Russia, he must still feel
vaguely, when he looks up at the starry heavens, that
there is a Power over him, upon Whom he is dependent.
Now if we, who are made for God, reject Him, we *must*
seek a substitute* for Him. We must have some earthly
object which so captivates us as to take the place in our
lives which God should have. We need something
toward which we can direct those characteristics of the
soul that are made for God. We *must* worship something. If we do not call upon God, we use some earthly
substitute for prayer. They *serve the creature rather
than the Creator.*

   If a bullet charged with sufficient power to carry it

The word here translated "substitute," recalls memories of the World
War to all Germans. It is the word used to characterize the inadequate
substitutes that military necessity, plus the Allied blockade, forced upon
the women, aged men and children behind the lines. This memory colors
Heim's use of the term here.

far into space, strikes a wall which is only a few feet
from the gun from which it is fired, the bullet will re-
bound with the same velocity energy and do great dam-
age. That is true also of the soul, which possesses a
yearning for eternity, an impulse that can find fulfill-
ment only in God. If it turn itself away from God, all
its energy is directed back to earth. This fact explains
the demonic passion frequently manifested in the ritual
of the non-Christian religions. When, on a holy day in
modern India, thousands of people have waited in silent
expectation for the climax of the festival which is
reached soon after sunset with the appearance of the
idol—perhaps an enormous silver figure of a bull with
the image of the god Siva on its back—and when this
idol surrounded by flaming torches, is borne through
the crowd, the mental attitude of the people is startlingly
transformed and swept by an insane enthusiasm. Everyone presses forward and seeks to touch the magic-work
ing image. The utmost confusion prevails while, everywhere, the cry is heard, "Siva, Siva, hear us!" It is a
stirring and tragic scene to see the fervor of surrender
to which human beings are capable, their capacity for
complete captivation and then to see how, if they do not
yield themselves to God, this capacity is directed toward
the worship of an inanimate idol. This misdirected
yearning for eternity also explains the strength of Communism. From this comes the amazing fanaticism with
which its adherents rage against things they formerly
considered sacred. It has often been said that Communism is the mystic religion of the Russian soul, but
acting with negative power. The same glow that once

burned in the Russian church is now directed against
God and, with incalculable hatred, seeks to destroy the
last remnant of its former faith.

But we need not seek the meaning of Paul's
words, *God also gave them up to uncleanness through
the lusts of their hearts,* in heathendom and in the anti-
Christian movements of our day. We can determine it
in our own hearts. Quite often we think that we can
adopt an attitude of benevolent neutrality toward
God. We do not want to sever relationship with Him,
neither do we wish to surrender ourselves to Him. We
would like to retain a point of authority within ourselves. But that were impossible, once we have no resting place within ourselves. At the same moment in
which we lose our prayer-contact with God, we fall victim to the lusts of our own heart. We are like an object
that lies on an inclined plane. Either there is a power
which holds it in place, or it rolls downward with ever
increasing rapidity. A few years ago at a mountain
station in central Germany some railway cars were separated from the rest of the train, through the carelessness
of the brakeman. For a moment, it seemed that the
oversight might be unattended by tragic results. But
the grade was steep and so the unfastened cars began to
roll. Vain attempts were made to stop them with the
handbrakes. Hurried telephone calls were made to sta-
tions below that barriers of earth and railroad ties might
be thrown up to check the downward rush of the cars.
But their ever-increasing momentum carried them
through all hindrances until they plunged over a cliff,
where they remained a twisted mass of wood and iron.

We experience something of a similar character when we lose the only thing which sustains us on the steep slope of life. At first it appears to be quite harmless for us to break off contact with God and follow our own desires. For a time, we still have control of ourselves. By strength of will we are able to master our feelings and maintain inner discipline. But very soon we reach a point at which we lose control. When we have once told a lie, our sense of truth is blunted. When we have lost control of our natural impulses, the power of gravity begins to work. We are no longer master of our own impure thoughts. Our desires become increasingly demanding. We are dragged down to depths hitherto undreamed of. God, from whom we have separated ourselves, gives us over to the lust of our heart. He delivers us over to the gravitational pull of our desires and the demanding claims of our natural impulses. Our thirst, which can never be satisfied, becomes greater and more terrible. We fall into the pit which opens within ourselves. We do not become aware of this through coarse, fleshly sins, alone. Those of us who have never done anything really bad and who feel ourselves quite safe, are threatened by the same deadly danger. If we give up our daily prayer contact with God, we do not, as we often suppose, remain at the same point. Since we are standing upon an inclined plane, almost before we are aware of it, we slip into the dark abysses of our own soul; a dangerous pride; a hard lovelessness; an unsatiable love of money; a feeling of bitterness against those who are better off than we are.

II.

If this is the condition in which we stand; if we fall
into the depths when we do not remain with God, then
there is for all of us but one possible question: Is there
a power that can stop this deadly fall, this descent into
the abyss that opens within ourselves? We cannot stop
ourselves if we have come to stand on this dangerous
descent. Our human wills can do much. At the beginning of a wrong course there is always the possibility
that a firm decision may turn in another direction.
But we draw nearer and nearer to the danger point
where the power of our will becomes inadequate. By
the rapids above Niagara Falls there stands, at a certain
place, a sign bearing this inscription, "Below this point,
no help can be given!" Until he reached this point a
strong swimmer might still be able to overcome the current and reach the shore in safety. Down to this point,
also, a speed-boat might be able to go, and still have
sufficient power to reverse its course. But below this
point there is no turning back. The current is too strong.
So it is in the inner development of every human being.
There is a place at which we are compelled to write:
"Below this point, no help can be given!" Here, the current which carries us downstream becomes too strong to
withstand. Here, our will-power becomes inadequate
and unavailing.

Nor can any other person, nor any other power in
this world restrain a human being who finds himself
upon this steep declivity. No pastor, teacher, faithful
friend, father or mother can hold a man back from im-
pending tragedy, if he has broken away from God. The

gravitational force is too strong. The desires and impulses of the natural man have asserted their mastery. We stand helpless before them, if we have lost our hold upon God.

But now we come upon the amazing fact which first changed the life of Paul from its very foundation and then made of him a missionary, because it was so great that he must tell other people about it. There is a *power unto salvation,* that is, a power which can stop the death plunge, which we ourselves cannot avert and which no other person nor power can hinder. There is a power which sustains us with invisible hands over the abyss that has opened within us and beneath us. What power is that? *I am not ashamed of the Gospel*—the joyful message—*of Christ: for it is the power of God unto salvation.* If this were a philosophy of life or a system of learning, there would be no reason to offer it to a world which, by an overwhelming majority, rejects it. The philosophies of life, these images which we throw upon the white wall of the unsolved mystery of the world, have changed from century to century. And when, today, we survey all these attempts to explain the world, that follow one another like scenes of a motion-picture film, we become sated and weary. It was not necessary for Paul to travel to the capital of the world with a new philosophy. Rome was a veritable market place of philosophic theories. What drove him to take his message to the world's capital in spite of all obstacles, was the fact that his Gospel was far greater than any philosophy. He brought no theories and imaginative systems, but *the power of God unto salvation.*

He came to testify of a power that was of equal importance to all men, because it alone could restrain the
deadly descent which threatens all mankind.

One cannot speak impersonally of a power. It is
possible to prove or to oppose a philosophic opinion
without any personal entanglement. But with a *power*
that is impossible. Of it, one can testify only as one
has himself felt its working. A power shows itself only
in action, that is to say, only in the object it has overcome. Only he can really speak of a power who has
withstood it, but whose opposition has been conquered.
Paul's entire *Epistle* to Rome is, from beginning to end,
the hymn of thanksgiving of a saved man, or rather, of
a whole congregation of saved men, who have experienced this power in their own lives. We today can speak
of this power in no other way. Only if we are saved
does the inner relationship of this act of salvation become clear to us. Our personal experience reveals that
which God has done to halt the death plunge of humanity. He sent a Savior to us, strong enough to face all the
forces which would destroy man. This Savior gave
Himself for us absolutely. His very life was given for
us. And not only that. He has entered into a relationship with us that is so secure that no other power is able
to take us out of His hand. For us, who are staggering
and helpless, there is only one possible salvation. We
must be united forever with Him who sustains us above
the pit of destruction.

In the Bay of Biscay a terrific storm resulted in a
wave sweeping a traveler from the deck of his ship. A
sailor sprang overboard immediately and, by straining

his body to the utmost, was able to bring the other man to the boat which had been quickly lowered. Then his strength gave out and he sank beneath the waters. His body was recovered and laid upon the deck of the ship he had trod shortly before. The man who had been saved fell upon his knees beside the corpse of his deliverer, kissed the cold, wet forehead and stiffened hands, and vowed that the whole of his future life must express the gratitude he would always feel. Because of what had been done for him, the traveler felt an inner relationship to his rescuer that could never be broken. A man, whose death has saved ours, binds us forever to him, because our thankfulness can never cease. But this is but a weak, human illustration of what has occurred between us and Christ. He leaped into the flood which was bearing us away from God and gave His life to save us from drowning in it. By this act He has bound us to Himself for ever. We have become His possession. His hands still hold us above the abyss into which we would fall, were He not supporting us. He bears us above the depths that are open about us and in us, like a lifeboat bears shipwrecked passengers over the mysterious ocean depths. Under us may be doubt, because the conditions of life have become unbearable and we can see no way of escape. Christ, Who has purchased us at such great cost, holds us with His invisible hands above the pit of doubt. Under us may be all the passions of a sinful human heart, the fervent wish for earthly happiness, for success and joy which we lack. If we were left to ourselves, we would fall irredeemably into these depths. But He sustains us over the rushing waters; beneath us

are the Everlasting Arms; invisible hands bear us over
the mysterious and insatiable depths of our hearts. Beneath us may be despondency, pessimism and weariness
of life, together with a dark anger because we are
among the disinherited of life. But we do not sink into
these dangerous moods. Christ supports us; for it is He
Who says of Himself, *And I give them eternal life; and
thoy shall nover perish, neither shall any man pluck
them out of my hand.*

If Jesus has this power, what consequences follow
for us? We, ourselves, need no longer struggle. We
need only doubt ourselves and remain with Him. We
need only to hold fast our relationship with Him. That
is what Paul means by *faith;* for faith means nothing
else than doubting oneself and clinging to Christ, Who
supports us above the abyss. Paul says that the new
righteousness comes *from faith to faith.* Every step of
the new life is a step of faith. It begins with faith, it
ends with faith. "He will fight for us, and we shall wait
quietly for Him."

Now we know why the message which Paul brings
applies to the whole world, and why we dare not keep
silent, even though all other men should reject the Gospel. It is a power which everyone needs if he is not to
sink, a power which is stronger than all those which
draw man downward. Murderers, who were shortly to
be executed, have been saved by this power, and have
ascended the scaffold as the children of God. Drunkards,
whose bodies have been veritably poisoned with alcohol
and who were beyond the help of any "cure", have become free men through this power. There is no condi-

tion for which it is not adequate. For it is no human power; it is the power of Almighty God *unto salvation to everyone that believeth.*

Why dare we, then, not retreat with this message of Christ? Not because the church still exercises a certain influence upon public life. That might soon change. Not because we still have noble and gifted men in our congregations who might still be able to influence our modern world. The church of God in its earliest days —days in which she was most vital—consisted, in many cities, almost exclusively of slaves. And such conditions might return. There is but one reason why we cannot be ashamed of the Gospel before the whole world. It is that all people, even in their rebellion against God, are still in His power. And God has given His weak follow- ers a priceless treasure, a power that can do what no man or earthly power can do. It is the power that can free a man from himself, can release him from the demons that are in him, and from the passions and cares which would drag him under if he were left to himself.

Not long ago, Prochanow, leader of the Protestant forces in Russia, related a significant and dramatic oc- currence. Two of the Bible messengers who, in spite of all the persecution of Christianity, still travel from place to place in certain sections of the country, stood preaching on a low hill in a certain village, with a num- ber of people gathered about them. Suddenly shots rang out and one of the preachers dropped to the ground mor- tally wounded. Everyone expected the other to quickly withdraw, to escape being shot down, also. But he did nothing of the kind. He knelt beside the body of his

168 *THE GLORY OF THE CROSS*

friend and prayed, took the Bible from the stiffening
hand of his dead comrade and continued to proclaim
the Gospel. This display of simple heroism made such
a deep impression upon the villagers, that a spiritual
awakening spread through the entire community.

The anti-Christian movement of our day seeks by
every possible means to silence the messengers of the
Gospel. But we dare not retreat, no matter how strong
the opposition may be; for we owe the Gospel even to
a world which persecutes and kills God's ambassadors.
As saved men, we are, even today, *debtor both to the
Greeks and to the barbarians, to the wise and to the un-
wise.*